INTRODUCING
ISSUES WITH
OPPOSING
VIEWPOINTS®

Drug Abuse

Lauri S. Friedman, *Book Editor*

GREENHAVEN PRESS
A part of Gale, Cengage Learning

GALE
CENGAGE Learning·

Detroit • New York • San Francisco • New Haven, Conn • Waterville, Maine • London

Elizabeth Des Chenes, *Managing Editor*

For more information, contact:
Greenhaven Press
27500 Drake Rd.
Farmington Hills, MI 48331-3535
Or you can visit our Internet site at gale.cengage.com

For product information and technology assistance, contact us at

Gale Customer Support, 1-800-877-4253
For permission to use material from this text or product, submit all requests online at
www.cengage.com/permissions

Further permissions questions can be e-mailed to permissionrequest@cengage.com

Articles in Greenhaven Press anthologies are often edited for length to meet page requirements. In addition, original titles of these works are changed to clearly present the main thesis and to explicitly indicate the author's opinion. Every effort is made to ensure that Greenhaven Press accurately reflects the original intent of the authors. Every effort has been made to trace the owners of copyrighted material.

Cover image © ejwhite/Shutterstock.com.

LIBRARY OF CONGRESS CATALOGING-IN-PUBLICATION DATA

Drug abuse / Lauri S. Friedman, book editor.
    p. cm. -- (Introducing issues with opposing viewpoints)
  Includes bibliographical references and index.
  ISBN 978-0-7377-5675-3 (hbk.)
  1. Drug abuse--Juvenile literature. 2. Drug abuse--United States--Juvenile literature.
  3. Drug legalization--Juvenile literature. I. Friedman, Lauri S.
  HV5801.D57763 2012
  362.290973--dc23
                                      2011036230

Printed in the United States of America
2 3 4 5 6 7 16 15 14 13 12

Contents

Foreword

Indulging in a wide spectrum of ideas, beliefs, and perspectives is a critical cornerstone of democracy. After all, it is often debates over differences of opinion, such as whether to legalize abortion, how to treat prisoners, or when to enact the death penalty, that shape our society and drive it forward. Such diversity of thought is frequently regarded as the hallmark of a healthy and civilized culture. As the Reverend Clifford Schutjer of the First Congregational Church in Mansfield, Ohio, declared in a 2001 sermon, "Surrounding oneself with only like-minded people, restricting what we listen to or read only to what we find agreeable is irresponsible. Refusing to entertain doubts once we make up our minds is a subtle but deadly form of arrogance." With this advice in mind, Introducing Issues with Opposing Viewpoints books aim to open readers' minds to the critically divergent views that comprise our world's most important debates.

Introducing Issues with Opposing Viewpoints simplifies for students the enormous and often overwhelming mass of material now available via print and electronic media. Collected in every volume is an array of opinions that captures the essence of a particular controversy or topic. Introducing Issues with Opposing Viewpoints books embody the spirit of nineteenth-century journalist Charles A. Dana's axiom: "Fight for your opinions, but do not believe that they contain the whole truth, or the only truth." Absorbing such contrasting opinions teaches students to analyze the strength of an argument and compare it to its opposition. From this process readers can inform and strengthen their own opinions, or be exposed to new information that will change their minds. Introducing Issues with Opposing Viewpoints is a mosaic of different voices. The authors are statesmen, pundits, academics, journalists, corporations, and ordinary people who have felt compelled to share their experiences and ideas in a public forum. Their words have been collected from newspapers, journals, books, speeches, interviews, and the Internet, the fastest growing body of opinionated material in the world.

Introducing Issues with Opposing Viewpoints shares many of the well-known features of its critically acclaimed parent series, Opposing Viewpoints. The articles are presented in a pro/con format, allowing readers to absorb divergent perspectives side by side. Active reading questions preface each viewpoint, requiring the student to approach the material thoughtfully and carefully. Useful charts, graphs, and cartoons supplement each article. A thorough introduction provides readers with crucial background on an issue. An annotated bibliography points the reader toward articles, books, and websites that contain additional information on the topic. An appendix of organizations to contact contains a wide variety of charities, nonprofit organizations, political groups, and private enterprises that each hold a position on the issue at hand. Finally, a comprehensive index allows readers to locate content quickly and efficiently.

Introducing Issues with Opposing Viewpoints is also significantly different from Opposing Viewpoints. As the series title implies, its presentation will help introduce students to the concept of opposing viewpoints and learn to use this material to aid in critical writing and debate. The series' four-color, accessible format makes the books attractive and inviting to readers of all levels. In addition, each viewpoint has been carefully edited to maximize a reader's understanding of the content. Short but thorough viewpoints capture the essence of an argument. A substantial, thought-provoking essay question placed at the end of each viewpoint asks the student to further investigate the issues raised in the viewpoint, compare and contrast two authors' arguments, or consider how one might go about forming an opinion on the topic at hand. Each viewpoint contains sidebars that include at-a-glance information and handy statistics. A Facts About section located in the back of the book further supplies students with relevant facts and figures.

Following in the tradition of the Opposing Viewpoints series, Greenhaven Press continues to provide readers with invaluable exposure to the controversial issues that shape our world. As John Stuart Mill once wrote: "The only way in which a human being can make some approach to knowing the whole of a subject is by hearing what can be said about it by persons of every variety of opinion and studying all modes in which it can be looked at by every character of mind. No wise man ever acquired his wisdom in any mode but this." It is to this principle that Introducing Issues with Opposing Viewpoints books are dedicated.

Introduction

The United States has some of the highest rates of illegal drug use in the world, and combating that problem, along with related health issues and crime, has been the focus of the war on drugs for more than twenty-five years. But as the twenty-first century pushes on, of growing concern is the use and abuse of chemicals and substances that are legal, cheap, and plentiful, yet share many of the same dangerous side effects as the most risky and hardcore illegal drugs.

One of the newest and most concerning drugs is a powder nicknamed "bath salts." This product contains the chemical methylenedioxypyrovalerone, which is abbreviated as MDPV. Sold under the names Ivory Snow, Red Dove, White Lightning, Vanilla Sky, and Purple Wave, bath salts are a stimulant and have similar effects as cocaine and methamphetamine. After snorting, smoking, injecting, or drinking the drug, users feel euphoric and have vivid, and often violent, hallucinations. Other reactions include intense paranoia, seizure, and death. Mark Ryan, director of the Louisiana Poison Center, describes bath salts' effect on a user in the following way: "If you take the very worst of some of the other drugs—LSD and Ecstasy with their hallucinogenic-delusional type properties, PCP with extreme agitation, superhuman strength and combativeness, as well as the stimulant properties of cocaine and meth—if you take all the worst of those and put them all together this is what you get. It's ugly."[1]

Virtually unheard of in 2009, by 2011 bath salts were linked to a slew of disturbing and violent incidents. In some cases users died from overdose, including a Mississippi woman in 2010 and an Illinois woman in 2011. At other times people under the influence of the drug killed others and/or themselves. In April 2011, for example, US Army sergeant David Stewart and his wife, Kristy Sampels, died in a homicide-suicide while high on bath salts. Stewart shot Sampels and then himself as they were being chased in a car by police. One of them had killed their five-year-old son, Jordan, that morning.

In Florida a man high on bath salts tore a police car's radar unit out of the car with his teeth; elsewhere in Florida severe hallucinations brought on by bath salt use caused a woman to attack her mother with a machete. Neil Brown, of Mississippi, slit his face and stomach repeatedly with a knife while high on bath salts. He survived his experience, but twenty-one-year-old Dickie Sanders, of Louisiana, did not: Three days after snorting bath salts he continued to suffer from severe hallucinations, hysteria, and delirium and eventually cut his throat and shot himself. Other users have suffered long-term mental damage and ongoing hallucinations.

These are but a few examples of the violent and deadly incidents that have stemmed from bath salt abuse. In 2010 various nationwide poison control centers received more than 300 calls about incidents related to bath salts. In just the first three months of 2011, however, more than 780 such calls and about 1,500 bath-salt-related emergency room visits were recorded. The fact that no poison control center calls were made between January and March in 2009 demonstrates both the newness and rapid increase in bath salt use.

Compounding the disturbing nature of these tragic and violent incidents is the fact that in most states bath salts are legal and easy to get. They are available over the counter in truck stops, tobacco shops, novelty and other kinds of stores, and they are not yet federally regulated. No identification or waiting period is required to buy them, and packets are as cheap as twenty dollars. They are bought and sold as casually and openly as T-shirts, food, or books might be. "There was no back-alley drug dealer; there were no lowered voices or code words—just a small-business owner making a sale," reported Mehmet Oz, MD, who bought packets of bath salts for an article he filed for *Time* magazine on the problem. "I am telling you today, first as a father and then as a doctor, that the ease of that transaction chilled me. Kids everywhere are in danger from this substance, and the threat is legal, cheap and very deadly."[2]

Oz's is among the growing chorus of voices calling to ban bath salts and other synthetic drugs that continue to be legal. Heeding this call, Indiana, Florida, Louisiana, and South Dakota had made bath salts illegal by mid-2011, and bans were under consideration in New Jersey, Maryland, Pennsylvania, Mississippi, California, and Hawaii. Still, critics such as physician Richard Saunders, Dickie Saunders's father, argue that the United States has been too slow to enact a federal ban on such substances. In fact, Great Britain, Finland, Australia, Germany, Denmark, and Sweden have all acted to ban or control

MDPV, and Saunders, Oz, and others think the United States should act immediately to do the same.

Yet others argue the threat from bath salts has been overstated, saying that the majority of users do not react severely. Furthermore, they claim bans on the substance are unnecessary and even violate certain freedoms. Randy Heine, the owner of Rockin' Cards and Gifts, a Florida store that sells bath salts, for instance, claims the chemicals he sells are no more hazardous than alcohol or other legal drugs. Heine warns that legislators and others seeking to ban bath salts will end up creating an underground market for them, which will in turn cause other problems. "These people are out to create crime," he said. "This product was legal yesterday. Today, it's illegal."[3] Heine and others say that the problem with any kind of drug prohibition is that authorities are unable to completely eradicate drug use; the best they have been able to do is drive drug use underground, which typically increases crime, violence, the spread of disease, and has other negative effects.

How the United States should respond to the burgeoning problem of legal yet dangerous substances is just one of the topics explored in *Introducing Issues with Opposing Viewpoints: Drug Abuse.* Students will also consider opposing arguments on which drugs are a serious problem, whether marijuana should be decriminalized, whether medical marijuana offers relief from illness, whether the United States should continue the war on drugs or adopt harm-reduction strategies, and other issues. Guided reading questions and essay prompts will help them articulate their own opinions on this constantly evolving topic.

Notes

1. Quoted in Amanda Gardner, "Hallucinogens Legally Sold as 'Bath Salts' a New Threat," *Business Week,* February 4, 2011. www.businessweek.com/lifestyle/content/healthday/649596.html.
2. Mehmet Oz, "'Bath Salts': Evil Lurking at Your Corner Store," *Time,* April 25, 2011. www.time.com/time/magazine/article/0.9171.2065249.00.html.
3. Quoted in Greg Allen, "Florida Bans Cocaine-Like 'Bath Salts' Sold in Store," National Public Radio, February 8, 2011. www.npr.org/2011/02/08/133399834/florida-bans-cocaine-like-bath-salts-sold-in-stores.

Chapter 1

Is Drug Abuse a Serious Problem?

Conflicting statistics about teen drug abuse have led to varying opinions concerning the extent of drug abuse by youths in the United States.

Drug Abuse Is Increasing

Lloyd D. Johnston, Patrick M. O'Malley, Jerald G. Bachman, and John E. Schulenberg

"Daily marijuana use increased significantly in . . . grades in 2010 . . . . There was a significant increase in heroin use using a needle among 12th graders."

The following viewpoint is taken from the annual Monitoring the Future survey, an ongoing study of the behaviors, attitudes, and values of American youth. Each year, the National Institute on Drug Abuse, part of the National Institutes of Health, surveys about fifty thousand eighth-, tenth-, and twelfth-grade students on their health and drug habits. In 2010 the survey found that American youth are increasingly using a wide variety of drugs and substances. Researchers recorded an increase in marijuana, Ecstasy, cigarette, heroin, and prescription drug use, and found steady use of other drugs, including LSD, PCP, and amphetamines. The authors conclude that drug abuse is on the rise in part because new drugs become available all the time and it is difficult to teach drug use consequences to young people who talk to each other mostly about drug use benefits.

Lloyd D. Johnston, Patrick M. O'Malley, Jerald G. Bachman, and John E. Schulenberg, "Monitoring the Future: National Results on Adolescent Drug Use; Overview of Key Findings, 2010," University of Michigan Institute for Social Research, February 2011. Reproduced by permission.

AS YOU READ, CONSIDER THE FOLLOWING QUESTIONS:
1. One in how many high school seniors is a daily or near-daily marijuana user, according to the survey?
2. By what percent did heroin use with a needle increase among twelfth graders in 2010?
3. What is the process of "generational forgetting" and what does it mean in the context of the viewpoint?

In recent years, the trends in drug use have become more complex, and thus more difficult to describe. A major reason for this increased complexity is that cohort [group] effects—lasting differences between different cohorts entering secondary school—have emerged, beginning with increases in drug use during the early 1990s. Such cohort effects mean that usage rates (and sometimes attitudes and beliefs about various drugs) reach peaks and valleys in different years for different grades. . . .

In 2008, we introduced a set of tables providing an overview of drug use trends for the *three grades combined* [eighth, tenth, and twelfth]. While there are important differences by grade, this approach gives a more succinct summary of the general nature of historical trends over the last several years. Later sections in this monograph deal separately with each class of drugs and provide data for each grade individually.

Substance Abuse Is on the Rise

The most important findings to emerge from the 2010 survey were the following: *Marijuana* use, which had been rising among teens for the past two years, continued to rise in 2010 in all prevalence periods for all three grades. This stands in stark contrast to the long, gradual decline that had been occurring over the preceding decade. Of relevance, perceived risk for marijuana has been falling in recent years. Of particular relevance, *daily marijuana use* increased significantly in all three grades in 2010; and stands at 1.2%, 3.3%, and 6.1% in grades 8, 10, and 12. In other words, nearly one in sixteen high school seniors today is a current daily, or near-daily, marijuana user.

After a decline of several years in perceived risk for *ecstasy*, which we had been warning could presage a rebound in use, its use does now appear to be rebounding.

Alcohol use, including *binge drinking*, continued its longer term decline among teens, reaching historically low levels in 2010. Use has been in a long-term pattern of decline since about 1980, with the interruption of a few years in the early 1990s in which alcohol use increased along with the use of cigarettes and almost all illicit drugs. Among 12th graders in 1980, 41% admitted to having five or more drinks in a row on at least one occasion in the two weeks prior to the survey (what we call binge drinking). This statistic fell to 28% by 1992, prior to the rebound in the 1990s, but has now fallen further reaching 23% in 2010—a marked improvement.

After decelerating considerably in recent years, the long-term decline in *cigarette* use, which began in the mid-1990s, came to a halt in the lower grades in 2010. Indeed, both 8th and 10th graders showed evidence of an increase in smoking in 2010, though the increases did not reach statistical significance. Perceived risk and subsequently disapproval had both leveled off some years ago.

Annual surveys show an increase in the abuse of most drugs by US high school youths.

Narcotic Use Is Still High

Because marijuana is by far the most prevalent drug included in the *any illicit drug* use index, an increase in prevalence occurred for that index as well as for marijuana. The proportions using *any illicit drug other than marijuana* had been declining gradually since about 2001, but no further decline occurred in 2010.

There was a significant increase in *heroin use using a needle* among 12th graders in 2010, with annual prevalence rising from 0.3% in 2009 to 0.7% in 2010. However, because there was no simultaneous change in use in the lower grades nor any change in attitudes or beliefs that might explain such a change, we believe there is a good possibility that the change is due to chance sample fluctuation.

Cocaine and *powder cocaine* use continued gradual declines in all grades in 2010, though the one-year change did not reach statistical significance. *Sedative* use and use of *narcotics other than heroin*, which are reported only for 12th graders, similarly continued their slow, non-significant declines in 2010. *Vicodin* use decreased significantly only among 12th graders in 2010, with annual prevalence falling from 9.7% in 2009 to 8.0% in 2010. Even at 8%, it remains one of the most widely used illicit drugs.

The use of quite a number of drugs held fairly steady in 2010. These included an index of the use of *any illicit drug other than marijuana, LSD, hallucinogens other than LSD* taken as a class, *PCP, crack cocaine, heroin* without using a needle, *OxyContin, amphetamines* (*Ritalin* and *Adderall* specifically), *methamphetamine, crystal methamphetamine, tranquilizers, cough and cold medicines* taken to get high, several so-called "club drugs" (*Rohypnol, GHB,* and *ketamine*), and *anabolic steroids*. Use of most of these drugs is at or below peak levels,

Student Drug Use Is Once Again on the Rise

After experiencing a sharp decline in the 1980s, student drug use rose early in the 1990s but then declined until 2008. Drug use increased once again in 2009 and 2010.

Percent of Students Who Used Any Illicit Drug in Lifetime

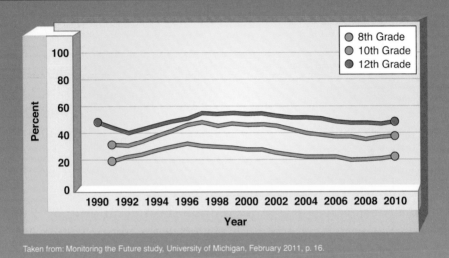

Taken from: Monitoring the Future study, University of Michigan, February 2011, p. 16.

in particular methamphetamine and crystal methamphetamine. In fact, annual use of methamphetamine is down in all three grades by between 60% and 80% since 1999, when its use was first measured. The drugs that are not down much from peak levels are the *narcotics other than heroin*; their continued high rate of use is among the more disturbing findings from the 2010 survey.

The Prescription Drug Problem

The misuse of psychotherapeutic *prescription drugs* (amphetamines, sedatives, tranquilizers, and narcotics other than heroin) has become a more important part of the nation's drug problem in recent years, in part because the use of most of these classes of drugs continued to increase beyond the point at which most illegal drugs ended their rise in the late 1990s, and in part because use of most of those same illegal drugs has declined appreciably since then. The proportion of

12th graders in 2010 reporting use of any of these prescription drugs without medical supervision in the prior year was 15.0%, up slightly from 14.4% in 2009 but a bit lower than in 2005, when it was 17.1%. Lifetime prevalence for the use of any of these drugs without medical supervision in 2010 was 21.6%. . . .

The Battle of Drug Education

Unfortunately, word of the supposed benefits of using a drug usually spreads much faster than information about the adverse consequences. The former—supposed benefits—takes only rumor and a few testimonials, the spread of which has been hastened greatly by the media and Internet. It usually takes much longer for the evidence of adverse consequences (e.g., death, disease, overdose, addiction) to cumulate and then be disseminated. Thus, when a new drug comes onto the scene, it has a considerable grace period during which its benefits are alleged and its consequences are not yet known. We believe that ecstasy is the most recent example of this dynamic.

To a considerable degree, prevention must occur drug by drug, because people will not necessarily generalize the adverse consequences of one drug to the use of others. Many beliefs and attitudes held by young people are drug specific. . . . These attitudes and beliefs are at quite different levels for the various drugs and, more importantly, often trend quite differently over time.

"Generational Forgetting" Helps
Keep the Epidemic Going

Another point worth keeping in mind is that there tends to be a continuous flow of new drugs onto the scene and of older ones being rediscovered by young people. Many drugs have made a comeback years after they first fell from popularity, often because young people's knowledge of their adverse consequences faded as generational replacement took place. We call this process "generational forgetting." Examples include LSD and methamphetamine, two drugs used widely in the 1960s that made a comeback in the 1990s after their initial popularity faded as a result of their adverse consequences becoming widely recognized during periods of high use. Heroin, cocaine, PCP, and crack are some others that have followed a similar pattern. At present, *LSD, inhalants,* and *ecstasy* are all showing the effects of generational forgetting—that is, perceived risk is declining appreciably for those drugs—which puts future cohorts at greater risk of having a resurgence in use. In the case of LSD, perceived risk among 8th graders has declined appreciably and more are saying that they are not familiar with the drug. It would appear that a resurgence in availability (which declined very sharply after about 2001, most likely due to the FDA's [US Food and Drug Administration's] closing of a major lab in 2000) could generate another increase in use.

EVALUATING THE AUTHOR'S ARGUMENTS:

The Monitoring the Future survey authors found that 15 percent of twelfth graders use prescription drugs without medical prescription; 6.1 percent use marijuana on a daily basis; and 0.7 percent use heroin with a needle. That means that in a class of about 300 students, 45 use prescription drugs, 18 use marijuana on a daily basis, and 2 use heroin. Think about what you know of the drug problem at your school. Do these numbers seem accurate? High? Low? Find out how many students are in your senior class and do the math based on these percentages. Then, state whether you think the numbers offer an accurate portrayal of drug abuse at your school.

Drug Abuse Is Declining

Institute for Behavior and Health

"The decline in illegal drug use is a major public health success and should be recognized as such."

The author of the following viewpoint is the Institute for Behavior and Health (IBH), whose mission is to identify and promote new strategies that will reduce the demand for illegal drugs. The IBH argues that drug abuse among American teens is, on the whole, declining. Even though certain sectors of youth continue to experiment with drugs, the IBH points out that the vast majority of teens do not use drugs. This is due to well-funded programs and policies that teach kids about the dangers of marijuana use, reduce the supply of drugs, and increase parental involvement. IBH concludes that America is winning the war against drug abuse.

The IBH is a nonprofit organization that was established in 1978.

AS YOU READ, CONSIDER THE FOLLOWING QUESTIONS:

1. What percent of the population aged twelve and older does the IBH say used illegal drugs in 1979? How does that compare with today's rates?
2. As cited in the viewpoint, how many billions of dollars does drug abuse cost the United States each year, according to the White House Office of National Drug Control Policy?
3. What is the Parents' Movement and what effect has it had on teen drug use, according to IBH?

"Combating Illegal Drug Use: We Are Succeeding," Institute for Behavior and Health, 2010. Reproduced by permission.

Today, there is good evidence that US drug prevention policies are working; 92% of those age 12 and over do not currently use any illegal drug, such as marijuana, heroin, methamphetamine or use prescription drugs nonmedically.

These facts speak to the measurable, yet incomplete, success of the US effort to combat illegal drug use:

- Illegal drug use in the US peaked in 1979 when 14.1% of the population age 12 and older were current users of illegal drugs.
- In 1992, illegal drug use in the US fell to a low of 6.7%.
- In 2008 illegal drug use rebounded to 8.0%.
- In terms of overall economic impact, in 2002, the White House Office of National Drug Control Policy (ONDCP) reported that the social costs of drug abuse are over $180.9 billion every year. This sum includes lost productivity, health care costs, and criminal justice expenditures for all illegal drugs combined. High as this is, the total cost is less than the social costs of either alcohol or tobacco alone.

The decline in illegal drug use is a major public health success and should be recognized as such. If this were any other type of public health problem, the decline of 43% in the rate of illegal drug use from 1979 to 2009 would be lauded as a remarkable achievement.

The National Effort to Reduce Drug Use

The 2010 National Drug Control Strategy released by the [Barack] Obama Administration and ONDCP is an extension and improvement of the ongoing US drug control policy. With emphases on reducing drugged driving, reducing prescription drug abuse, and improving and expanding community prevention, the National Strategy sets ambitious goals to reduce illegal drug use. Through these impressive new efforts, illegal drug use can and will be reduced below the current levels.

Never before the past 40 years in world history has any entire population been exposed to an almost limitless variety of dependence-producing drugs in high potency and by intensely rewarding routes of administration (particularly snorting, smoking and shooting). This drug epidemic has become a global burden. Responding to this threat

Abuse of Certain Drugs Has Declined

In 2010 America's twelfth graders reported lower use of inhalants, LSD, and cocaine (including crack) than in previous years.

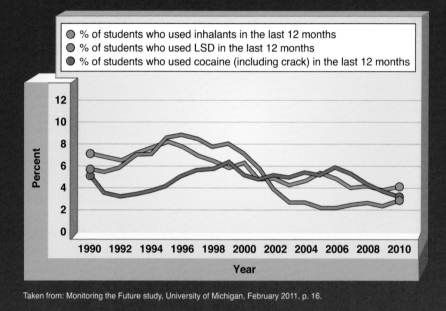

- ● % of students who used inhalants in the last 12 months
- ● % of students who used LSD in the last 12 months
- ● % of students who used cocaine (including crack) in the last 12 months

Taken from: Monitoring the Future study, University of Michigan, February 2011, p. 16.

is a serious public policy challenge, one that the US has met by a remarkable investment in a strategy that balances more traditional law enforcement with a new and very large investment in treatment, prevention and research. This bipartisan strategy has produced real but modest gains including the dramatic turndown in the overall level of illegal drug use from the peak of the epidemic in 1979.

One of the most significant factors in the decision by youth to use or not to use drugs is their perception of the harm that could come from using drugs. The perceived risk of using marijuana—the gateway illegal drug—is a pivotal factor. . . . Those who advocate for the normalization or legalization of marijuana claim that it is harmless. They discount the growing body of research that indicates that serious mental and physical damage is caused by the use of marijuana. The current federal government interagency campaign cautions about the dangers of smoking marijuana, especially for young people, whose still developing brains are particularly vulnerable to its effects. This information is vital to the country's efforts to reduce illegal drug use.

Drug Use Is Declining Among High School Students

The rate of marijuana use among high school seniors (a bell-wether indicator) fell 61% between 1978 and 1992. The use of drugs other than marijuana fell 71% during that time. Since this time, the use of both has begun to gradually increase.

The increase in drug use rates from 1992 to 1997 was the direct result of well-funded non-governmental pro-drug efforts to turn around the public's beliefs and attitudes toward illicit drug use. In the last few years there has been a newly energized national response at the grassroots and federal policy levels that seeks to protect youth from the use of the drugs by showing that illegal drug use, particularly marijuana use, is not a harmless, casual lifestyle choice.

Demand Reduction and Supply Reduction: A Winning Policy Combination

Demand reduction efforts reduce the demand for illegal drugs using prevention, treatment, and research. Supply reduction makes drugs scarcer, more expensive, and less socially tolerated.

For the past 35 years, US drug policy has been a balance of supply reduction (law enforcement) and demand reduction (treatment, prevention and research). The vociferous opponents of this strong combination call for the removal of the law enforcement side of this strategy, claiming that the nation's policy choice is *either* law enforcement or treatment. Nothing could be farther from the truth. It is the combination of both that brings success. Many people who receive drug abuse treatment in the US today do so *because* law enforcement requires them to be in treatment. Cutting out the long arm of the law would, in one blow, significantly reduce the number of individuals in drug treatment. What is needed for the future is not a choice between law enforcement or treatment, but rather new polices that unite law enforcement and treatment to work together more effectively over long periods of time.

Supply reduction is an effective tool for demand reduction because when drugs cost more and are more difficult to obtain there are fewer drug users and less demand for illegal drugs. Demand reduction is also an effective tool in supply reduction because when the number of drug users falls, drug supply falls correspondingly as the market for illegal drugs shrinks. Linking these complementary approaches maximizes the impact of the national strategy on illegal drug use by attacking the drug economy from both sides.

Between 1978 and 1992, marijuana use by high school seniors declined by 61 percent.

While this one-two punch has worked well in the past, the best hope for future reductions lies in improved and more cost-effective demand reduction. If the demand for illegal drugs remains high, then the money spent by would-be drug users would sustain a large supply of illegal drugs no matter how effective the supply reduction becomes. The search for what can be called *real demand reduction* is the heart of tomorrow's drug prevention policy.

Success of the Parents' Movement

The significant fall in illegal drug use in the US between 1979 and 1992 can be traced to many factors. A key factor was the impact of a national coalition started in the 1970s known as the Parents' Movement. During the 1980s [First Lady] Nancy Reagan embraced the message of the Parents' Movement with her "Just Say No" campaign. During the Administration of President George H.W. Bush, this anti-drug leadership was strongly supported. While this effective effort to de-normalize illegal drug use has often been seen as politically partisan, it was never a partisan movement. The manifesto of the Parents' Movement was written by Marsha Manatt, the sister of the then-National Chairman of the Democratic Party. The Parents' Movement received White House support when President Jimmy Carter's second Drug Czar, Lee Dogoloff, took up the cause. General Barry McCaffrey, President Bill Clinton's White House Drug Czar, also was a strong supporter of the Parents' Movement, as were many other Democrats. IBH encourages today's parents to look back and learn from the success of the Parents' Movement that was so effective in the 1970s and 1980s. Reinvigorating the Parents' Movement for the twenty-first century would provide organization, energy and education that is essential to success against drug abuse.

The Movement suffered neglect after 1992, leaving a marked void in leadership for drug abuse prevention. Without the organized efforts of committed parents, illegal drug use rates again rose sharply. Once mocked by some experts and officials, the Parents' Movement remains an inspiring testimony to the power of a relatively small, focused and dedicated group of people. Their experience demonstrates that "ordinary" parents are an extraordinary resource in preventing and treating drug abuse.

EVALUATING THE AUTHOR'S ARGUMENTS:

In the previous viewpoint the Monitoring the Future survey authors argued that drug use among teens is increasing because of data they found. For example, 6.1 percent of twelfth graders use marijuana on a daily basis, which is more than used the year before. But in this viewpoint the Institute for Behavior and Health points out that even if 6.1 percent of twelfth graders use marijuana daily, nearly 94 percent do not, and they consider that to be evidence that drug prevention policies are working. How do you interpret these statistics? Do you think they indicate there is a serious drug abuse problem, or not? Explain your reasoning and state with which author you ultimately agree.

Prescription Drug Abuse Is Skyrocketing

"Although prescription drugs can be powerful allies, they also pose serious health risks related to their abuse, which can lead to addiction and to death."

Nora D. Volkow

In the following viewpoint Nora D. Volkow argues that the problem of prescription drug abuse is growing at an alarming rate. She explains that prescription drug abuse has grown in several sectors of society, particularly among teens and young adults. This is worrisome, argues Volkow, because prescription drug abuse has serious health consequences, including dependency, cognitive decline, overdose, coma, organ trauma or failure, and even death. Prescription drug abuse also costs the nation in treatment, emergency room visits, and other services. For all of these reasons Volkow concludes that prescription drug abuse is a growing problem that needs to be addressed.

Volkow is director of the National Institute on Drug Abuse at the National Institutes of Health.

Nora D. Volkow, "Testimony to the Congressional Caucus on Prescription Drug Abuse," nida.nih.gov, September 22, 2010.

AS YOU READ, CONSIDER THE FOLLOWING QUESTIONS:
1. What factors have contributed to the increase in prescription drug abuse, according to Volkow?
2. How many emergency department visits in 2008 does Volkow say were due to misuse of prescription pain relievers?
3. What percent of eighteen- to twenty-five-year-olds say they used prescription drugs for a nonmedical purpose within the last month, according to the author?

In 2009, 7 million Americans reported current (past month) non-medical use of prescription drugs—more than the number using cocaine, heroin, hallucinogens, and inhalants combined. National surveys show that the number of new abusers of several classes of prescription drugs increased markedly in the United States in the 1990s, continuing at high rates during the past decade—abuse of prescription drugs now ranks second (after marijuana) among illicit drug users. Perhaps even more disturbing, approximately 2.2 million Americans used pain relievers nonmedically for the *first time* in 2009 (initiates of marijuana use were 2.4 million).

So what is behind this high prevalence and incidence? As expected, the motivations vary by age, gender, and other factors, which also likely include greater availability. The number of prescriptions for some of these medications has increased dramatically since the early 90's: more than 8-fold for stimulants, and 4-fold for opioids. Other contributors may be a consumer culture amenable to taking a pill for what ails you and the perception that abusing prescription drugs is less harmful than illicit ones. This is not the case: prescription drugs act directly or indirectly on the same brain systems affected by illicit drugs; thus their abuse carries substantial abuse and addiction liabilities and can lead to a variety of other adverse health effects. . . .

Troubling Signs of a Growing Problem

Selected indicators of the prescription drug and OTC [over-the-counter] medication abuse in this country include the following:

- Treatment admissions for opiates other than heroin rose from 19,870 in 1998 to 111,251 in 2008, over a 450-percent increase.

- The number of fatal poisonings involving prescription opioid analgesics more than tripled from 1999 through 2006, outnumbering total deaths involving heroin and cocaine.
- The Drug Abuse Warning Network (DAWN), which monitors emergency department (ED) visits in selected areas across the Nation, estimates that in 2008, roughly 305,000 ED visits involved nonmedical use of prescription pain relievers; 19,000 involved CNS [central nervous system] stimulants; and 325,000 involved CNS depressants (anxyiolytics, sedatives, and hypnotics). Over half involved more than one drug. These numbers have more than doubled for pain relievers, and nearly doubled for stimulants and CNS depressants since 2004.
- ED visits related to zolpidem (Ambien)—one of the most popular prescribed non-benzodiazepine hypnotics in the United States—also more than doubled during this period, from about 13,000 in 2004 to about 28,000 in 2008.

The abuse of prescription drugs is on the rise, and it now ranks second after marijuana in illicit drug use.

Who Is Abusing Prescription Drugs?

Latest trends show that adolescents and young adults may be especially vulnerable to prescription drug abuse, particularly opioids and stimulants.

Data from the 2009 National Survey on Drug Use and Health (NSDUH) indicate that rates of prescription drug use were highest among young adults 18 to 25, with 6.3 percent reporting nonmedical use in the past month. That said, earlier data on past-year *users* of any prescription psychotherapeutic drug, prevalence of dependence or abuse is higher for the 12–17 year-old age group than for young adults (15.9 vs. 12.7 percent). In this youngest age group, females exceed males in the nonmedical use of *all* psychotherapeutics, including pain relievers, tranquilizers, and stimulants, and are more likely to be dependent on stimulants.

Moreover, according to the Monitoring the Future survey (MTF), prescription and over-the-counter drugs comprised 8 of the top 14 categories of drugs abused by 12th graders in 2009. And while many medications can be abused, opioids display particularly disturbing abuse rates. The MTF shows, for example, that the rate of nonmedical use of Vicodin and OxyContin has remained unchanged for several years, with nearly 1 in 10 high school seniors reporting nonmedical use of the former and 1 in 20 of the latter.

Also of concern is the diversion of stimulants, particularly ADHD [attention-deficit/hyperactivity disorder] medications among students, who are using them to increase alertness and stay awake to study. The growing number of prescriptions written for this diagnosis has led to dramatically greater availability of stimulant medications with potential for diversion. For those who take these medications to improve properly diagnosed mental disorders, they can markedly enhance a patient's quality of life. However, prescription stimulants are increasingly being abused for nonmedical conditions or situations (e.g., to get high; as a cognitive enhancer), which poses potential health risks, including addiction, cardiovascular events, and psychosis.

Why Do They Do It?

The far-ranging scope of prescription drug abuse in this country stems not only from the greater prescribing of medications, but also from misperceptions of their safety when used nonmedically or by someone other than the prescription recipient. Among the latter, many are taking prescription drugs for their intended purposes, such as to relieve pain in the case of prescription opioids, or to enhance alertness in the case of ADHD medications but without a doctor's supervision. Indeed, students and even some parents see nothing wrong in the abuse of stimulants to improve cognitive function and academic performance. In fact, being in college may even be a risk factor for greater use of amphetamines or methlyphenidate nonmedically, with reports of students taking pills before tests and of those with prescribed medications being approached to divert them. Pain relievers show a similar link with regard to access, evidence also suggesting that parents sometimes provide their children with prescription medications to relieve their discomfort. When asked how prescription narcotics (opioids) were obtained for nonmedical use, more than half of 12th-graders said they were given the drugs or bought them from a friend or relative.

> **FAST FACT**
>
> In 2010 the Monitoring the Future survey conducted by the National Institute on Drug Abuse found that approximately 30 percent of tenth graders said it was "fairly" or "very" easy to acquire prescription drugs such as OxyContin.

Nonmedical use among children and adolescents is particularly troublesome given that adolescence is the period of greatest risk not only for drug experimentation but also for developing addiction. At this stage the brain is still developing, and exposure to drugs could interfere with these carefully orchestrated changes. Research also shows adolescents abusing prescription drugs are twice as likely to have engaged in delinquent behavior and nearly three times as likely to have experienced an episode of major depression as teens who did not abuse prescription medications over the past year. Finally, several studies link the illicit use of prescription drugs with increased rates of cigarette smoking, heavy drinking, and marijuana and other illicit drug use in adolescents and young adults in the United States. Thus, prescription drug abuse may be part of a pattern of harmful behaviors engaged in by those at risk for substance use and other mental disorders.

Prescription Drugs Commonly Abused by Teens

Of the fourteen most frequently abused drugs among twelfth graders, eight are prescription and over-the-counter drugs.

Percentage of Past-Year Drug Use Among Twelfth Graders, by Drug

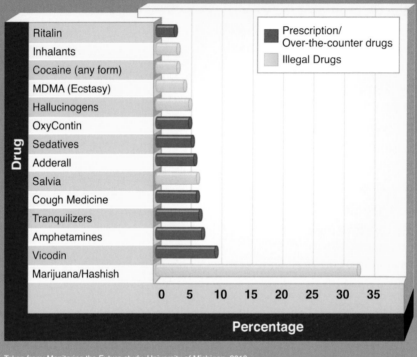

Taken from: Monitoring the Future study, University of Michigan, 2010.

Older adults represent another area of concern. For although this group currently comprises just 13 percent of the population, they account for more than one-third of total outpatient spending on prescription medications in the United States. Older patients are more likely to be prescribed long-term and multiple prescriptions, which could lead to misuse (i.e., *unintentionally* using a prescription medication other than how it was prescribed) or abuse (i.e., *intentional* nonmedical use).

Various reasons underlie why older adults may misuse or abuse prescription drugs. Cognitive decline, combined with greater numbers of medications and complicated drug-taking regimens may lead to unintentional misuse. Alternatively, those on a fixed income may intentionally use another person's remaining medication to save money. Because older adults also experience higher rates of other illnesses as well as normal changes in drug metabolism, it makes sense that even moderate abuse or unintentional misuse of prescription drugs by elderly persons could lead to more severe health consequences. Therefore, physicians need to be aware of the possibility of abuse and to discuss the health implications with their patients and/or their caretakers. . . .

Prescription drug abuse is not a new problem, but one that deserves renewed attention. It is imperative that as a nation we make ourselves aware of the consequences associated with abuse of these medications. For although prescription drugs can be powerful allies, they also pose serious health risks related to their abuse, which can lead to addiction and to death. It will be a question of balance so that people suffering from chronic pain, ADHD, or anxiety can get the relief they need while minimizing the potential for abuse.

EVALUATING THE AUTHOR'S ARGUMENTS:

Nora D. Volkow is director of the National Institute on Drug Abuse, the government organization charged with combating drug addiction and abuse in the United States. The author of the following viewpoint, Jim Gogek, is a journalist who has written about research-based solutions to alcohol, tobacco, and drug problems for twenty years and has worked as communications director for a national substance abuse research institute. How do the authors' backgrounds inform your opinion of their arguments? Are you more inclined to trust one over the other? Why or why not? Explain your reasoning.

The Extent of Prescription Drug Abuse Is Exaggerated

Jim Gogek

"I'm not saying that painkiller abuse is not a problem. It is. But there are much, much bigger problems in the world of alcohol, tobacco and other drugs."

In the following viewpoint Jim Gogek argues that prescription drug abuse is not the most pressing concern in the world of substance abuse prevention. Tobacco and alcohol abuse injure and kill millions more people each year than prescription drugs, he says. Therefore, Gogek contends, those issues should receive more of the prevention community's attention and funding than prescription drug abuse does. Although the misuse of prescription drugs is a problem, Gogek says it is covered excessively by the media, who want to put a fresh and exciting spin on drug abuse stories. In reality, says Gogek, prescription drugs are important and save lives, and millions of people would suffer if their access to them were restricted. He concludes that the substance prevention community should focus their efforts on the substances that are the most harmful, even if they are not as novel or interesting as newer problems.

Jim Gogek, "Is Painkiller Abuse Really the Most Important Recovery Story? Hint: No, It's Not," atodblog.com, August 25, 2010. Reproduced by permission.

Gogek is a journalist who has written about research-based solutions to alcohol, tobacco, and drug problems for twenty years. He has worked as a communications director for a national substance-abuse research institute and as a director of an underage-drinking-prevention program. He also sits on the board of the San Diego chapter of the American Lung Association of California.

AS YOU READ, CONSIDER THE FOLLOWING QUESTIONS:
1. How many people died in 2010 from tobacco-related issues, according to Gogek? How many from alcohol?
2. What is an "iatrogenic effect" and what does it mean in the context of the viewpoint?
3. Why is Gogek unconcerned that painkiller abuse experienced a 400 percent increase from 1998 to 2008?

It's National Recovery Month, or will be in a few days, and health reporters and bloggers are looking for something "new" to write about recovery. The prevailing belief is that if it's not "new," it's not news. I prefer a definition that includes the most important current events, not just the newest.

Many feel that the problem of prescription drug abuse has been exaggerated, since tobacco and alcohol abuse kill millions more people each year than prescription drugs do.

Anyway, this year [2010], in case you couldn't tell, the big news in recovery is painkiller abuse. Celebrity deaths provided a natural lead-in.

There Are Bigger Problems than Prescription Drug Use

I'm not saying that painkiller abuse is not a problem. It is. But there are much, much bigger problems in the world of alcohol, tobacco and other drugs. The problem with those bigger problems is that they're timeless classics and the media wants new. So, each year, the communications folks at government agencies and big public health nonprofits pull their hair out trying to figure out how they can keep the media interested in addiction, which is important.

This year, the painkiller abuse story feeds the beast. (Better than a few years back when the big story was Ecstasy, though use was very low).

But really what are the big stories this year? Try these:
- More than 5 million people will die this year around the world from tobacco, and that number will rise to 8 million by 2030.
- More than 400,000 of those deaths will be in the United States.
- Alcohol will kill 2.5 million people worldwide, and an estimated 76.3 million people currently have alcohol use disorders. In the United States, alcohol will kill about 75,000 people a year through disease, violence and unintentional injuries.
- Attempts to build an effective system of treatment and prevention for alcohol, tobacco and other drugs will be a worldwide failure yet again this year.

We Need a Sensible Approach to Prescription Drugs

When you're reading stories about painkiller abuse, and as calls for a crackdown get louder, keep in mind a Greek-rooted phrase called the iatrogenic effect, or "harm from the cure."

Many people really need painkillers. We don't want people in severe pain because they can't get medicine. We don't want senior citizens who need Percocets to not get them. The head of the American Cancer Society recently said that worldwide, people need more access to painkillers, not less. He called the current lack of access "shameful."

More People Seek Treatment for Alcohol Than for Any Other Drug

Alcohol treatment admissions continue to dominate, indicating that more people struggle with alcohol abuse and addiction than any other substance, including prescription drugs such as painkillers.

Substances for which most recent treatment was received in the past year among persons aged 12 or older:

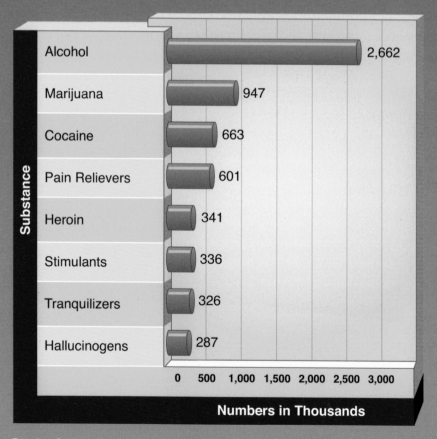

Substance	Numbers in Thousands
Alcohol	2,662
Marijuana	947
Cocaine	663
Pain Relievers	601
Heroin	341
Stimulants	336
Tranquilizers	326
Hallucinogens	287

Numbers in Thousands

Taken from: Substance Abuse and Mental Health Services Administration, *Results from the 2008 National Survey on Drug Use and Health: National Findings*, 2009.

So this is not a simple subject about passing new laws or instituting a crackdown.

Some news stories have focused on "pill mills," and I'm sure there will be more of that, with dead celebrity b-roll [video-footage] thrown in. I'm concerned that with excessive media attention, painkillers will become an enforcement issue instead of a medical one. And state lawmakers will get way too involved in drug prescription criteria, which is happening right now in the state of Washington. What we need are doctors who understand pain *and* addiction, and who will make sensible diagnoses concerning both problems.

Focus on the Biggest Substance Abuse Problems

You may be hearing that you should be very worried about painkiller abuse because of a 400 percent increase from 1998 to 2008 in treatment admissions. But take a look at the chart. Alcohol treatment admissions are still more than four times higher.

And [don't forget about] all these tobacco users. Nearly 24 percent of the US population is still smoking. Those problems—and the global failure to treat and prevent substance dependence and abuse—are what National Recovery Month should be about.

> ## EVALUATING THE AUTHOR'S ARGUMENTS:
>
> In this viewpoint Jim Gogek uses facts, statistics, examples, and reasoning to make his argument that the problem of prescription drug abuse has been exaggerated. He does not, however, use any quotations to support his point. If you were to rewrite this article and insert quotations, what authorities might you quote? Where would you place the quotations, and why?

Performance-Enhancing-Drug Abuse Is a Serious Problem in Sports

"Side effects specific to males include increased breast size, baldness, shrunken testicles and infertility. Females are at risk of baldness, increased body hair and a deeper voice."

Lisa Sweetingham

In the following viewpoint Lisa Sweetingham discusses the problem of performance-enhancing-drug abuse in the United States. She explains that several high-profile baseball players have been caught using such drugs, which compromises the integrity of professional sports and sends a dangerous message to kids, who typically idolize sports heroes. Sweetingham argues that famous athletes make performance-enhancing drugs look cool and effective, but in reality such drugs have severe side effects and health risks. She urges parents to use the crisis of performance-enhancing drugs in professional sports as an opportunity to tell their children that performance-enhancing drugs are dangerous and not worth the risk.

Sweetingham is a journalist whose work has appeared in the *New York Times, Parade, Spin,* and the *Los Angeles Times,* where this viewpoint was originally published.

AS YOU READ, CONSIDER THE FOLLOWING QUESTIONS:
1. When were anabolic-androgenic steroids first used for performance enhancement, according to Sweetingham?
2. Name at least five side effects the Mayo Clinic says are associated with performance-enhancing-drug use.
3. Who is Bob Hazelton and how does he factor into the author's argument?

I'm not a huge baseball fan. I don't know what all the stats mean or how many home runs away from Godlike status Alex Rodriguez [A-Rod] might be. But when left fielder Manny Ramirez rolled into town last year [2008], Dodger fever struck. I became a regular reader of the Sports pages of this newspaper [*Los Angeles Times*] and discovered ESPN on the TV remote. And I was charmed to learn that a friend's 8-year-old daughter, a Pony League All-Star slugger, had taped pictures of Ramirez to her bedroom wall when most girls her age covet the Jonas Brothers.

All that Manny love turned cold last week after he was suspended for 50 games for violating Major League Baseball's [MLB's] drug policy—bad news that came just days after allegations that A-Rod may have been juicing as early as high school and during his time as a Yankee.

Performance-Enhancing Drugs Are Like Other Dangerous Drugs

As a journalist, I've spent several years hanging out with drug dealers and drug cops to cover the trade, and I suspect that the reasons people take performance-enhancement drugs aren't so different from why they take cocaine or Ecstasy. They want to be better, sexier, more heroic versions of themselves. Bob Hazelton wanted that too, but more about him later.

Anabolic-androgenic steroids, which can be injected or taken orally, are synthetic derivatives of testosterone and have been used in clinical practice since the 1940s for burns, surgery, radiation therapy and, since the 1980s, for treatment of cancer and AIDS-associated wasting syndrome. Their earliest documented use for performance enhancement was in the 1950s, by Soviet weightlifters.

Major League Baseball Suspensions

At least 29 Major League Baseball players had been suspended for steroid use as of May 2011.

Player Name	Team	Suspension Type
Alex Sanchez	Tampa Bay Devil Rays	10 Days
Jorge Piedra	Colorado Rockies	10 Days
Agustin Montero	Texas Rangers	10 Days
Jamal Strong	Seattle Mariners	10 Days
Juan Rincon	Minnesota Twins	10 Days
Rafael Betancourt	Cleveland Indians	10 Days
Rafael Palmeiro	Baltimore Orioles	10 Days
Ryan Franklin	Seattle Mariners	10 Days
Mike Morse	Seattle Mariners	10 Days
Carlos Almanzar	Texas Rangers	10 Days
Felix Heredia	New York Mets	10 Days
Matt Lawton	New York Yankees	10 Days
Jose Guillen	Kansas City Royals	15 Games
Jay Gibbons	Baltimore Orioles	15 Games
Neifi Perez	Detroit Tigers	25 Games
Ryan Jorgenson	Cincinnati Reds	25 Games
Mike Cameron	San Diego Padres	25 Games
Yusaku Iriki	New York Mets	50 Games
Jason Grimsley	Arizona Diamondbacks	50 Games
Guillermo Mota	New York Mets	50 Games
Juan Salas	Tampa Bay Devil Rays	50 Games
Sergio Mitre	New York Yankees	50 Games
J.C. Romero	Philadelphia Phillies	50 Games
Manny Ramirez	Los Angeles Dodgers	50 Games
Pablo Ozuna	Philadelphia Phillies	50 Games
Edinson Volquez	Cincinnati Reds	50 Games
Ronny Paulino	Florida Marlins	50 Games
Neifi Perez	Detroit Tigers	80 Games
Manny Ramirez	Tampa Bay Rays	100 Games

Taken from: Baseball-Almanac.com, May 4, 2011. www.baseball-almanac.com/legendary/steroids_baseball.shtml.

Serious Health Risks from Steroid Use

But in the last 30 years, usage has spread beyond elite athletes, who sought to secretly enhance their competitiveness, and into the realm of individuals who seek greater self-perceived attractiveness. Amateurs and athletes are equally at risk for side effects that, according to the Mayo Clinic, include liver abnormalities and tumors, high cholesterol, aggressive behavior, depression and severe acne. For adolescents, there is an additional risk of stunted growth.

Side effects specific to males include increased breast size, baldness, shrunken testicles and infertility. Females are at risk of baldness, increased body hair and a deeper voice—all of which recall the saga of Heidi Krieger, the 1986 former East German shot-put champion who was fed such high doses of steroids by her coaches that, in 1997,

The earliest documented use of performance-enhancing drugs was by Soviet weightlifters in the 1950s.

she gave in to her stunning metamorphosis, underwent a sex change operation and became Andreas Krieger.

Experts say chronic steroid abusers add "accessory" medications to their performance-enhancement cocktail. Though one steroid might make your muscles bigger, you'll need another to get that lean, cut look. Throw in some Tamoxifen to help prevent breast enlargement, Viagra for sexual dysfunction and human chorionic gonadotropin—the drug that got Ramirez banned—to revive testosterone levels. The list goes on when one's desire to get bigger, faster and stronger knows no bounds.

The Disturbing Story of One Man's Addiction

Steroids aren't physically addictive, but their psychologically addictive properties are well known to researchers. Hamsters will self-administer testosterone directly to their brains even to the point of death. As for humans? Former heavyweight boxer Bob Hazelton testified in tears before Congress in 2004 about his addiction.

Hazelton began using in 1970. By 1985, he was spending $200 to $300 a week and took as much as 1,400 milligrams a day of a drug whose therapeutic dose was closer to 5 or 10 milligrams a day. In 1986, after suffering from debili-

FAST FACT

New Jersey, Texas, and Illinois are the only three states that mandate state-wide random steroid testing of student athletes.

tating heart attacks and blood clots, his left leg was amputated below the knee. He kept on doping. A year later, his right leg was amputated. He quit using and started speaking out, from his wheelchair, about the dangers of steroid abuse.

Hazelton's story still gets to Joseph Rannazzisi, deputy assistant administrator in the Drug Enforcement Administration's [DEA's] office of diversion control, who also testified that day. Rannazzisi is a pharmacist by training and a drug agent by trade, and he works closely with Major League Baseball to share information, technical advice and trends in the illegal use of anabolic steroids. For the record, the DEA thinks MLB is doing a decent job of making players accountable.

"I think they're doing everything they can to identify people who are abusing performance-enhancement drugs, not only to protect the integrity of baseball but also to protect the health and safety of players," Rannazzisi says.

The DEA isn't interested in singling out players for prosecution, but it is targeting the organizations that distribute steroids for non-medical use.

A Bad Message to Kids

As a father of five, Rannazzisi admits that he cares deeply about whether professional sports players are doping. "In addition to it being a violation of the law, it sends a bad message to our kids," he says.

Thankfully, according to the latest Monitoring the Future study, 91% of American 12th-graders disapprove of steroids, and just 2.2% report having ever used them.

Manny's fall from grace at least provides an opportunity to discuss the dangers of performance-enhancement drugs with our children.

"I'd never say to my own kids that somebody is bad or evil because they've done something like that," Rannazzisi says. "What I'd say is, 'He's made a mistake, and we don't want you to make that same mistake.'"

Which is pretty much what my friend told his daughter on their way to a Dodger game. She was disappointed at first, but she shrugged it off and focused on the other players. I might follow her lead. I never cared about the stats anyway. So, Manny, when you return in July, if you can stay off the juice, I'll keep reading the Sports section.

EVALUATING THE AUTHOR'S ARGUMENTS:

In this viewpoint Lisa Sweetingham argues that performance-enhancing-drug use should be discouraged in sports because of the negative message athletes' use of the drugs send to young fans. How do you think Norman Fost, author of the following viewpoint, would respond to this claim? Write two to three sentences on how you think he might argue the point. Then, state with which author you agree, and why.

Viewpoint

6

Performance-Enhancing-Drug Use Should Be Allowed in Sports

"The selective paternalism behind the ban on steroids would not be tolerated in other walks of life."

Norman Fost

In the following viewpoint Norman Fost argues that professional athletes should be allowed to use performance-enhancing drugs. He argues that competitive athletes have, throughout history, used a variety of tactics to improve their performance. In his opinion, performance-enhancing drugs are just the latest enhancement technology, no different from athletic equipment made from high-tech material, specially processed food, or the massive funding that gives some teams an edge over others. Fost claims that performance-enhancing drugs are not as physically risky as some critics have stated. He also points out that Americans routinely allow people in high profile positions to take risks for the sake of their work. For all these reasons he concludes that performance-enhancing drugs have a legitimate place in modern sports.

Fost is professor of pediatrics and bioethics at the University of Wisconsin and director of the school's Bioethics Program, which he founded in 1973. He has published widely on ethical and legal issues in health care and served on numerous federal committees, including President Bill Clinton's Health Care Task Force.

AS YOU READ, CONSIDER THE FOLLOWING QUESTIONS:
1. Who is Lyle Alzado and how does he factor into Fost's argument?
2. What does the author say athletes have in common with police, military, and construction workers? How does this comparison support his argument?
3. Why, in Fost's opinion, does performance-enhancing-drug use *not* threaten the credibility of an athlete's record?

Since the beginning of recorded history, competitive athletes have tried to enhance their performance in every way imaginable. Naked Greeks put on shoes. Babylonians used herbs. Kenyans trained at high altitude. American swimmers used greasy swimsuits. Marathoners loaded their bodies with carbohydrates. But none of these enhancing technologies has created the hysteria surrounding anabolic steroids and human growth hormone (HGH).

There Is Always an "Unfair Advantage" in Sports

What are the claims of those who would condemn elite athletes or send them to prison for trying to maximize their performance? The simple answer is that they are breaking the rules, or in some cases, the law. But the rules depend on arguments or claims that are morally incoherent, hypocritical, or based on ice-cold wrong information.

Critics assert that athletes who use performance-enhancing drugs have an unfair advantage. But an advantage is only unfair if it is not equally available. This is usually solved by equalizing access, not by prohibition. The hypocrisy is everywhere. The same year [Olympic sprinter] Ben Johnson was vilified for using drugs that were by all accounts widely available, Janet Evans, the American swimmer, boasted about the greasy swimsuits that the Americans had kept secret from their competitors. Bud Selig, the commissioner of baseball, preaches about a level playing field but tolerates a system in which the Yankees spend two to four times as much as all but a few competitors.

Health Risks Are Overstated

Critics assert that steroids and HGH cause life-threatening harm, but the claims are wildly exaggerated or simply made up. Lyle Alzado, Exhibit A for the perils of steroids, died of a brain tumor, but there is not a single medical source showing any association between his tumor and steroids.

We are told repeatedly that steroids cause heart disease and strokes but it is hard to identify a single elite athlete who suffered either calamity while using steroids.

HGH has been given to half a million children for decades and there is little evidence of any serious harm. In fact, the major risk of these drugs is caused by the policies of driving them underground, manufactured in unknown conditions with no oversight by regulatory agencies, and no possibility of careful studies to assess the benefits and risks.

The selective paternalism behind the ban on steroids would not be tolerated in other walks of life. More athletes have died playing professional baseball than from using steroids, and the deaths related to playing football are 10–100 times higher than those from steroids, but the games go on. We allow competent adults to take on life threatening risks from construction, police work, or joining the army, where the prospects of death are dramatically higher than even the inflated claims about steroids.

> **FAST FACT**
>
> A March 2009 study published in the *American Journal of Physical Medicine & Rehabilitation* found that more than 9 percent of retired National Football League players said they had used steroids at one point during their careers. Among linemen, the rates were higher: 16.3 percent of offensive linemen and 14.8 percent of defensive linemen admitted this.

Critics claim that steroids and human growth hormone can cause life-threatening harm. Professional football player Lyle Alzado (pictured) blamed steroid use for his inoperable brain tumor, but no link has been found between steroid use and such tumors.

Drug Use Does Not Undermine the Game

Critics assert that steroids and HGH are unnatural, but there is not an elite athlete anywhere who competes without unnatural assistance, nor is it coherent to argue that eating natural potatoes out of the ground is morally superior to carbo-loading from factory made pasta.

Critics assert that performance-enhancing drugs undermine the support of fans, but attendance at major league baseball games has never been higher than in what is widely known as the steroid era, and Barry Bonds, the perfect villain, is the greatest attraction in sports in the past decade. Mark McGwire and Sammy Sosa are widely considered to have "saved" baseball following an embarrassing strike, and McGwire admitted at the time to using androstenedione, a steroid precursor, for the explicit purpose of enhancing his performance.

Devotees bemoan the loss of credibility in new records enhanced by drugs. But contemporary records cannot be compared to previous accomplishments for many reasons unrelated to drugs. In baseball, the fences are shorter, the pitching mound is lower, the ball is said to be livelier, the strike zone has changed, and some games are played at a mile high stadium. By one calculation, if Babe Ruth played in today's stadiums, his home run total would have been closer to 1,000 than the mere 700+ achieved by Henry Aaron and Barry Bonds.

A Universal Goal and Behavior

Enhancing performance is a universal goal and behavior. The most valuable service a pediatrician provides is the enhancement of the immune system of perfectly normal children. Others rely on coffee, cars, or computers to achieve life goals. If there is something immoral about any of this, sufficient to justify the witch-hunt that characterizes the current situation, the argument has yet to be made.

EVALUATING THE AUTHOR'S ARGUMENTS:

Norman Fost argues that athletes who use performance-enhancing drugs are no different from athletes who get an advantage from wearing special shoes, training at high altitude, or using fast swimsuits. What do you think—is he right? Are performance-enhancing drugs no different from other performance-enhancing tactics? Or are they fundamentally different, and worse, somehow? Explain your position and quote in your answer from at least one text you have read.

Chapter 2

Should Marijuana Be Decriminalized?

Much of the controversy surrounding the decriminalization of marijuana is tied to its increasing use for medical purposes.

Marijuana Is a Dangerous Drug

National Institute on Drug Abuse

> *"Evidence suggests that a person's risk of heart attack during the first hour after smoking marijuana is four times his or her usual risk."*

The National Institute on Drug Abuse (NIDA) is the government organization charged with combating drug addiction and abuse in the United States. In the following viewpoint NIDA argues that marijuana is a dangerous drug. The agency warns there are multiple physical and psychological effects from marijuana smoking, including memory loss and increased risk for cancer and heart attack. Long-term marijuana use might also be associated with mental illness, including psychosis, warns NIDA. Marijuana use also affects a person's potential for success: The agency reports that smokers of marijuana typically complete fewer years of schooling and earn less money than people who do not. For all of these reasons, NIDA concludes that marijuana is a risky and dangerous drug.

AS YOU READ, CONSIDER THE FOLLOWING QUESTIONS:
1. In how many 2008 emergency department visits was marijuana a contributing factor, according to NIDA?
2. How does marijuana compare with tobacco regarding the amount of irritants and carcinogens it contains, as cited in the viewpoint?
3. What did a study among postal workers find about employees who tested positive for marijuana use, according to NIDA?

"Marijuana Abuse," National Institute on Drug Abuse, September 2010.

Marijuana is the most commonly used illicit drug (15.2 million past-month users) according to the 2008 National Survey on Drug Use and Health (NSDUH). That year, marijuana was used by 75.6 percent of current illicit drug users (defined as having used the drug some time in the 30 days before the survey) and was the *only* drug used by 53.3 percent of them. . . .

The Drug Abuse Warning Network (DAWN), a system for monitoring the health impact of drugs, estimated that in 2008, marijuana was a contributing factor in over 374,000 emergency department (ED) visits in the United States, with about two-thirds of patients being male, and 13 percent between the ages of 12 and 17. . . .

Psychosis and Memory Loss Among Side Effects of Marijuana

Marijuana users who have taken large doses of the drug may experience an acute psychosis, which includes hallucinations, delusions, and a loss of the sense of personal identity. Although the specific causes of these symptoms remain unknown, they appear to occur more frequently when a high dose of cannabis is consumed in food or drink rather than smoked. Such short-term psychotic reactions to high concentrations of THC are distinct from longer-lasting, schizophrenia-like disorders that have been associated with the use of cannabis in vulnerable individuals. . . .

An enduring question in the field is whether individuals who quit marijuana, even after long-term, heavy use, can recover some of their cognitive abilities. One study reports that the ability of long-term heavy marijuana users to recall words from a list was still impaired 1 week after they quit using, but returned to normal by 4 weeks. However, another study found that marijuana's effects on the brain can build up and deteriorate critical life skills over time. Such effects may be worse in those with other mental disorders, or simply by virtue of the normal aging process.

Increased Risk of Heart Attack

Within a few minutes after inhaling marijuana smoke, an individual's heart rate speeds up, the bronchial passages relax and become enlarged, and blood vessels in the eyes expand, making the eyes look red. The heart rate—normally 70 to 80 beats per minute—may increase by 20 to 50 beats per minute, or may even double in some cases. Taking other drugs with marijuana can amplify this effect.

Limited evidence suggests that a person's risk of heart attack during the first hour after smoking marijuana is four times his or her usual risk. This observation could be partly explained by marijuana raising blood pressure (in some cases) and heart rate and reducing the blood's capacity to carry oxygen. Such possibilities need to be examined more closely, particularly since current marijuana users include adults from the baby boomer generation, who may have other cardiovascular risks that may increase their vulnerability.

A Toxic Mixture

The smoke of marijuana, like that of tobacco, consists of a toxic mixture of gases and particulates, many of which are known to be harmful to the lungs. Someone who smokes marijuana regularly may have many of the same respiratory problems that tobacco smokers do, such as daily cough and phlegm production, more frequent acute chest illnesses, and a greater risk of lung infections. Even infrequent marijuana use can cause burning and stinging of the mouth and throat, often accompanied by a heavy cough. One study found that extra sick days used by frequent marijuana smokers were often because of respiratory illnesses.

FAST FACT

The Substance Abuse and Mental Health Services Administration reports that 62 percent of Americans who used marijuana before they were fifteen years old have used cocaine at some point, but only about 0.6 percent of Americans who have never used marijuana have ever used cocaine.

In addition, marijuana has the *potential* to promote cancer of the lungs and other parts of the respiratory tract because it contains irritants and carcinogens—up to 70 percent more than tobacco smoke. It also induces high levels of an enzyme that converts certain hydrocarbons into their cancer-causing form, which could accelerate the changes that ultimately produce malignant cells. And since marijuana smokers generally inhale more deeply and hold their breath longer than tobacco smokers, the lungs are exposed longer to carcinogenic smoke. However, while several lines of evidence have suggested that marijuana use may lead to lung cancer, the supporting evidence is inconclusive. The presence of an unidentified active ingredient in cannabis smoke having protective properties—if corroborated and properly characterized—could help explain the inconsistencies and modest findings. . . .

Like tobacco smoke, marijuana smoke contains a toxic mixture of gases, carcinogens, and particulates that are known to have harmful effects on the lungs.

Is There a Link Between Marijuana Use and Mental Illness?

Research in the past decade has focused on whether marijuana use actually causes other mental illnesses. The strongest evidence to date suggests a link between cannabis use and psychosis. For example, a series of large prospective studies that followed a group of people over time showed a relationship between marijuana use and later development of psychosis. Marijuana use also worsens the course of illness in patients with schizophrenia and can produce a brief psychotic reaction in some users that fades as the drug wears off. The amount of drug used, the age at first use, and genetic vulnerability can all influence this relationship. One example is a study that found an increased risk of psychosis among adults who had used marijuana in adolescence *and* who also carried a specific variant of the gene for catechol-O-methyltransferase (COMT), an enzyme that degrades neurotransmitters such as dopamine and norepinephrine.

In addition to the observed links between marijuana use and schizophrenia, other less consistent associations have been reported between marijuana use and depression, anxiety, suicidal thoughts among adolescents, and personality disturbances. One of the most frequently cited, albeit still controversial, is an amotivational syndrome, defined as a diminished or absent drive to engage in typically rewarding activities. Because of the role of the endocannabinoid system in regulating mood, these associations make a certain amount of sense; however, more research is needed to confirm and better understand these linkages. . . .

Users Operate at a Reduced Intellectual Level

Research has shown that marijuana's negative effects on attention, memory, and learning can last for days or weeks after the acute effects of the drug wear off. Consequently, someone who smokes marijuana daily may be functioning at a reduced intellectual level most or all of the time. Not surprisingly, evidence suggests that, compared with their nonsmoking peers, students who smoke marijuana tend to get lower grades and are more likely to drop out of high school. A meta-analysis of 48 relevant studies—one of

A 2011 poll found that Americans of all political persuasions oppose the legalization of marijuana.

Question: "Do you favor or oppose the legalization of marijuana?"

Political Persuasion	Favor %	Oppose %	Unsure %
ALL	41	56	2
Democrats	42	56	2
Independents	48	49	3
Republicans	28	70	2

Figures may not be exact, due to rounding.

Taken from: CNN/Opinion Research Corporation poll, April 9–10, 2011.

the most thorough performed to date—found cannabis use to be associated consistently with reduced educational attainment (e.g., grades and chances of graduating). However, a *causal* relationship is not yet proven between cannabis use by young people and psychosocial harm.

That said, marijuana users themselves report poor outcomes on a variety of life satisfaction and achievement measures. One study compared current and former long-term heavy users of marijuana with a control group who reported smoking cannabis at least once in their lives but not more than 50 times. Despite similar education and income backgrounds, significant differences were found in educational attainment: fewer of the heavy users of cannabis completed college, and more had yearly household incomes of less than $30,000. When asked how marijuana affected their cognitive abilities, career achievements, social lives, and physical and mental health, the majority of heavy cannabis users reported the drug's negative effects on all of these measures. In addition, several studies have linked workers' marijuana smoking with increased absences, tardiness, accidents, workers' compensation claims, and job turnover. For example, a study among postal workers found that employees who tested positive for marijuana on a pre-employment urine drug test had 55 percent more industrial accidents, 85 percent more injuries, and a 75-percent increase in absenteeism compared with those who tested negative for marijuana use.

EVALUATING THE AUTHOR'S ARGUMENTS:

The National Institute on Drug Abuse (NIDA) and Jim Hightower and Phillip Frazer, authors of the following viewpoint, agree that marijuana is the most widely used illicit drug in the United States. They disagree, however, on what this means about marijuana's danger. Hightower and Frazer conclude that marijuana's popularity is evidence of its safety; NIDA argues that the widespread use of marijuana has troubling physical, mental, social, and financial consequences. After considering the arguments in both viewpoints, with which author(s) do you agree on the extent to which marijuana is dangerous? List at least two pieces of evidence that swayed you.

Marijuana Is Not a Dangerous Drug

"While marijuana cannot be said to be completely harmless— what product is?—neither is it the dangerous bugaboo it is portrayed to be."

Jim Hightower and Phillip Frazer

In the following viewpoint Jim Hightower and Phillip Frazer argue that marijuana is not dangerous and that the war against marijuana does much more harm than marijuana itself. They explain that marijuana has been the victim of a mass smear campaign that began in 1914, when it was first demonized by savvy entrepreneurs and misinformed government officials. Since then the United States has spent billions of dollars harassing citizens, imprisoning them, and scaring them with myths and lies about the drug. In reality, say Hightower and Frazer, marijuana is much less dangerous than legal substances such as alcohol. It has few health risks, does not negatively or permanently alter a user, and has become so mainstream that even presidents have admitted to using it. The authors explain that many states are relaxing their laws or decriminalizing marijuana, which further proves it is not dangerous. The authors conclude that marijuana is not a dangerous drug and should be legalized.

Jim Hightower and Phillip Frazer, "Time to Stop America's Preposterous War on Pot: The 'Drug War' Is Doing Far More Harm than Marijuana Itself Ever Will," *The Hightower Lowdown*, vol. 11, no. 11, November 2009. Reproduced by permission.

Hightower is a radio commentator, writer, speaker, and syndicated columnist. Hightower and Frazer are coeditors of *The Hightower Lowdown,* an e-newsletter about marijuana and related issues.

AS YOU READ, CONSIDER THE FOLLOWING QUESTIONS:
1. What is *Reefer Madness* and how does it factor into the authors' argument?
2. Someone is arrested on marijuana charges every how many seconds, according to Hightower and Frazer?
3. Which thirteen states do the authors say have decriminalized the possession of marijuana?

You might remember Robert McNamara's stunning *mea culpa* [admission of fault] delivered a quarter century after his Vietnam War policies sent some 50,000 Americans (and even more horrendous numbers of Vietnamese) to their deaths in that disastrous war. In his 1995 memoir, the man who had been a cold, calculating secretary of defense for both [John] Kennedy and [Lyndon] Johnson belatedly confessed that he and other top officials had long known that the war was an unwinnable, ideologically driven mistake. "We were wrong," he wrote, almost tearfully begging in print for public forgiveness. "We were terribly wrong."

Yes, they were, and so are today's leaders (from the White House to nearly all local governments), who are keeping us mired in the longest, most costly, and most futile war in U.S. history: the drug war. . . .

The Demonization of Marijuana

In 1914, newspaper magnate William Randolph Hearst mounted a yellow-journalism crusade to demonize the entire genus of cannabis plants. Why? To sell newspapers, of course, but also because he was heavily invested in wood-pulp newsprint, and he wanted to shut down competition from paper made from hemp—a species of cannabis that is a distant cousin to marijuana but produces no high. Hearst simply lumped hemp and marijuana together as the devil's own product, and he was not subtle about generating public fear of all things cannabis. As reported in the August [2009] issue of *Mother*

Jones magazine, Hearst's papers ran articles about "reefer-crazed blacks raping white women and playing 'voodoo satanic' jazz music."

Actually, marijuana was largely unknown in America at the time and little used, but its exotic name and unfamiliarity made it an easy target for fearmongers. The next wave of demonization came in 1936 with the release of an exploitation film classic, *Reefer Madness*. It was originally produced by a church group to warn parents to keep their children in check, lest they smoke pot—a horror that, as the film showed, would drive kids to rape, manslaughter, insanity, and suicide.

Then Congress enthusiastically climbed aboard the anti-pot political bandwagon, passing a law that effectively banned the production, sale, and consumption of marijuana. Signed by FDR [President Franklin Delano Roosevelt] on August 2, 1937, this federal prohibition remains in effect today. Although it has been as ineffectual as Prohibition, the 1919–1933 experiment to stop people from consuming "intoxicating liquors," this ban continues, despite its staggering cost and dumfounding destructiveness.

The Unfair and Wasteful War on Weed

Consider a few facts about America's weed war:

- It diverts hundreds of thousands of police agents from serious crimes to the pursuit of harmless tokers, including agents from the local and state police, FBI, Drug Enforcement [Administration], and U.S. Marshals, Secret Service, Border Patrol, Customs, and Postal Service.
- By even the most conservative estimate, the outlay from us taxpayers now tops $10 billion a year in direct spending just to catch, prosecute, and incarcerate marijuana users and sellers, not counting such indirect costs as militarizing our border with Mexico in a hopeless effort to stop marijuana imports.
- Police agents at all levels trample our Bill of Rights in their eagerness to nab pot consumers by conducting illegal car searches, phone and email taps, garbage scrounging, and door-busting night raids.
- Even people who are merely suspected of marijuana violations and have had no charges filed against them can (and regularly do) have their cars, money, computers, and other property confiscated by

police. In a reversal of America's fundamental legal principles, it is up to these suspects to prove that their property is "innocent" of any crime.

- People convicted of possessing even one ounce of marijuana can face *mandatory* minimum sentences of a year in jail, and having even one plant in your yard is a federal felony.
- 41,000 Americans are in federal or state prisons right now on marijuana charges, not counting people in city and county jails.
- Police arrest someone in America every 36 seconds on marijuana charges. A record-setting 872,720 of these arrests were made in 2007—more than for all violent crimes combined—and seven million Americans have been arrested since 1995.
- 89% of all marijuana arrests are for simple possession of the weed, not for producing or selling it. . . .

Marijuana Is Too Popular to Be as Bad as Is Claimed

Hitting yourself over the head one time with a ball-peen hammer could be considered an experiment. Doing it twice, though, would be stupid. And doing it repeatedly is insane.

The war on weed is insane, for our officials keep sacrificing tax dollars, lives, civil liberties, and their own credibility in a "terribly wrong" and losing effort. They've been whacking us for decades with ever-bigger and more-repressive prohibition hammers, but marijuana availability and use keep going up, not down.

The 2008 survey on drug use conducted by the Department of Health and Human Services (HHS) shows pot to be popular with millions of Americans. Of those surveyed, 41% admit to

> **FAST FACT**
>
> According to the 2009 *National Survey on Drug Use and Health,* about 104 million Americans aged twelve or older have tried marijuana at least once in their lifetimes. That is more than 41 percent of the US population aged twelve and older.

having partaken at some point in their lives, 10% enjoyed it in the past year, and 6% use it regularly. These numbers greatly understate the actual level of marijuana consumption, because the survey is taken by federal health agents going door-to-door for in-person interviews. In effect, they're asking, "Have you been consuming an illicit drug—an activity that violates federal law and is punishable by a long prison term?" Many choose to fib.

Well, say Washington's die-hard weed warriors, it's really about protecting America's youth, deterring them from the evils of pot. Good luck with that. Ask practically any teenager, and you'll learn that marijuana is readily available to them—in a 2005 survey, 85% of high-school seniors said it was "easy to get." Because kids don't need an ID to get an ounce of pot, it's even easier to get than alcohol, which is a regulated drug. Last year's HHS drug-use survey found that 15% of 14-to-15-year-olds have taken tokes, as have 31% of the 16-to-17-year-olds. By age 20, 45% of adolescents have tried marijuana. . . .

Few Health Problems Compared with Alcohol

Over the years, the anti-reefers have cemented myths (a.k.a. lies) in the popular culture to demonize the product—including sensational claims that marijuana is more addictive than cigarettes, causes lung cancer, leads users to heroin, produces schizophrenia, and makes your teeth fall out. Such claims are ludicrous and have been soundly refuted by numerous independent scientific studies, but the media rarely covers these uncolorful truths.

While marijuana cannot be said to be completely harmless—what product is?—neither is it the dangerous bugaboo it is portrayed to be. As a typical scientific study concluded in 2002, "The high use of cannabis is not associated with major health problems for the individual or society." Indeed, it poses nowhere near the health dangers of alcohol—yet no one proposes to destroy breweries or imprison people for drinking martinis. . . .

Marijuana Is Mainstream

Such conservative icons as [economist] Milton Friedman, [political commentator] William F. Buckley, Jr., and [former secretary of state] George Schultz have been unabashed advocates of rethinking pot prohibition. The mayor of New York City, the governor of California, and rising numbers of politicos between the two coasts no longer fear owning up

Viewpoint author Jim Hightower speaks before a crowd. He and coauthor Phillip Frazer contend that the government has misled the American public by lying about and demonizing marijuana.

to a pot past. Also, we've now elected three presidents in a row who were known tokers in their earlier days. (In admitting the deed, they progressed from [Bill] Clinton's slippery "I didn't inhale" to [Barack] Obama's candid "I inhaled. That was the point.")

Several TV shows, including the widely acclaimed "Mad Men," portray characters using marijuana as matter-of-factly as those sipping wine. One hit show, unblinkingly titled "Weeds," is about a suburban pot-dealing mom. Another indicator of marijuana's movement into the cultural mainstream is the emergence of "stiletto stoners." Featured on the "Today Show" and in popular magazines, these are successful professional women who unapologetically prefer to wind down after work with a joint instead of a cosmopolitan.

Public-opinion polls are also reflecting this major shift in attitudes: 55% say possession of personal amounts of marijuana should not be criminal (Gallup, 2005); 78% support doctor-prescribed medical marijuana (Gallup, 2005); 51% say alcohol is more dangerous than marijuana and only 19% think the opposite (Rasmussen, August

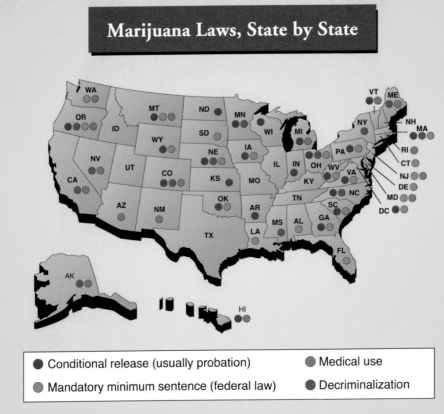

Marijuana Laws, State by State

Conditional release (usually probation)

Mandatory minimum sentence (federal law)

Medical use

Decriminalization

Taken from: National Organization for the Reform of Marijuana Laws (NORML), 2011.

2009); more than 75% say the drug war is a failure (Zogby, 2008); and 52% say marijuana should be legal, taxed, and regulated—while only 37% disagree (Zogby, May 2009).

Relaxed Laws Prove Marijuana Is Not Dangerous

As attitudes are changing, so are repressive laws. Pushed by grassroots activists (and basic logic), state and local governments have begun walking step by step away from the weed war. Since 1996, 13 states—from Rhode Island to Alaska—have passed laws (most by majority vote in initiative elections) to allow the growing and distribution of doctor-prescribed marijuana for medical purposes.

More recently, a move has been sweeping the country to decriminalize the mere possession of marijuana—a small fine might be issued (like a traffic ticket), but there are no criminal penalties. Pot possession is no longer criminalized in 13 states: Alaska, California, Colorado,

Maine, Massachusetts, Minnesota, *Mississippi(!),* Nebraska, Nevada, New York, North Carolina, Ohio, and Oregon.

Other changes include initiatives passed in Albany, Denver, Missoula [Montana], Seattle, and the state of Oregon mandating that police make pot possession and public consumption one of their lowest enforcement priorities. Drug reformers are also succeeding in Louisiana, Michigan, New York, and Washington state to scale back the harsh mandatory sentences for marijuana violations.

The most recent move is for outright legalization. The concept here is straightforward: treat marijuana the same as we do booze—i.e., turn its production, sale, and consumption into activities that are legal, regulated, and taxed.

EVALUATING THE AUTHOR'S ARGUMENTS:

The previous viewpoint was written by the National Institute on Drug Abuse (NIDA), the government agency charged with combating drug addiction and abuse in the United States. The authors of the viewpoint you just read, Jim Hightower and Phillip Frazer, say that the government has lied, exaggerated, misrepresented, or otherwise misinformed the American public about the dangers of marijuana. After reading both viewpoints, which author do you trust more on this issue, NIDA or Hightower-Frazer? Why? Explain your reasoning and quote from at least one of the texts in your answer.

Viewpoint
3

The Risks of Medical Marijuana Outweigh the Benefits

Mehmet Oz and Mike Roizen

"Using pot instead of real medical care just isn't smart."

In the following viewpoint Mehmet Oz and Mike Roizen argue that medical marijuana poses more health risks than health benefits. They say there is no evidence to show that medical marijuana helps improve many of the conditions it is purported to aid. Furthermore, most people who take medical marijuana smoke it, which puts them at increased risk of heart attack, weakened immunity, lung damage, and other disorders that are more serious than the ones they initially seek treatment for. Finally, Oz and Roizen say, smokers of medical marijuana send the wrong message to teens about what constitutes medicine and what constitutes responsible treatment of disease.

Oz and Roizen are both doctors. Oz is vice chair of surgery and professor of cardiac surgery at Columbia University. Roizen is chair of the Division of Anesthesiology, Critical Care Medicine, and Pain Management at the Cleveland Clinic. They have coauthored the book *You: On a Diet*.

AS YOU READ, CONSIDER THE FOLLOWING QUESTIONS:
1. For what diseases do Oz and Roizen say there is no evidence to prove that marijuana helps?
2. What is inhaling deep lungfuls of marijuana equivalent to, according to the authors?
3. What effect do the authors say marijuana has on one's immune system?

D on't let boutique-style dispensaries and a respectable new name—medical marijuana—blow smoke in your eyes. Yes, marijuana has solid credentials for relieving some serious problems (cancer pain, nausea, anorexia and tough-to-ease nerve pain). But can a pot-infused lemon bar or a hand-rolled

Jars of marijuana are stored at a medical marijuana clinic. The authors say that many patients using medical marijuana try to take low doses of the drug to reduce its harmful side effects.

joint improve everything from high blood pressure to diabetes and Alzheimer's disease?

Not likely.

Marijuana Is Not Real Medicine

The herb's transformation into an all-purpose healer has gotten way out of hand. Among our concerns: Using pot instead of real medical care just isn't smart. There's no good evidence that it helps high blood pressure, diabetes and Alzheimer's, not to mention osteoporosis, sleep apnea and drug-resistant bacterial infections.

When medical marijuana is a good choice, treat it like any drug: Aim to minimize the side effects. Start by taking pill forms instead of lighting up. Inhaling deep lungfuls delivers more carcinogens and toxic chemicals than up to 20 cigarettes. It also dumps as much tar into your lungs as four cigarettes and causes inflammation that can make it harder to fight cancer.

Other risks: *Heart strain.* In the hour after you smoke a joint, the danger of a heart attack rises five-fold, say researchers from Boston's Beth Israel Deaconess Medical Center. Pot boosts levels of a compound called apolipoprotein III that keeps fats stuck in your bloodstream and it revs up your heart rate.

> **FAST FACT**
>
> According to the Drug Abuse Warning Network, marijuana was involved in about 37.7 percent of all drug-related emergency room visits in 2008.

Medical Marijuana Has Serious Risks

Brain drain. Many people who use medical marijuana responsibly try to keep doses low (or use pills instead) to avoid the highs, spaciness and brain fog you get from smoking it. They're smart. In one study, people with multiple sclerosis who smoked marijuana were 50 percent slower on a mental-processing test than nonsmokers.

Weakened immunity. THC, the ingredient that eases pain and makes you high, is also a powerful immune-system downer. In a new study, it triggered tidal wave increases of "myeloid-derived suppressor

"Mrs Preston, you have to understand that medicinal marajuana is not something that I can prescribe lightly. It's not a matter of being 'square'."

cells." What they suppress is your immune system, which can boost your risk for all sorts of infections, encourage existing cancers and throw a monkey wrench into cancer treatments. If your immunity is already compromised, be wary.

Lung damage. Since people tend to inhale pot smoke long and deeply, smoking three to four joints a day may cause as much lung damage as smoking a pack of cigarettes. Long-term use doubles your odds for coughing, wheezing and chronic bronchitis.

Consider Safer Alternatives

So what are the safer alternatives? Start with the prescription pills that contain marijuana's active ingredients, particularly synthetic THC. Yes, we know they often aren't strong enough to ease cancer pain, nerve pain, MS muscle spasticity and AIDS-related nerve pain the way the real thing can.

Also, try eating your medicine instead of smoking it. Mix marijuana into baked goods or, if you live in a state where medical marijuana is legal, buy your supply at a marijuana bakery. Or consider a vaporizer, which in essence releases marijuana "smoke"; if you inhale the vapors, you get the active ingredients with fewer toxins, research suggests.

Send a Healthy Message to Young People

Skipping the joints (in favor of other forms) also sends a healthier message to the young people in your life about smoking in general and marijuana in particular. Teens who smoke pot have more detrimental, long-term brain effects than adults, and the new hype that weed's just another home remedy doesn't help.

> **EVALUATING THE AUTHOR'S ARGUMENTS:**
>
> Mehmet Oz and Mike Roizen, the authors of this viewpoint, are both doctors. How does this affect your opinion of their arguments? Are you more likely to believe what they say on this issue? Do you think that, in general, doctors are always to be trusted when it comes to issues like medical marijuana? Why or why not?

Viewpoint
4

The Benefits of Medical Marijuana Outweigh the Risks

Paul Armentano

"Cannabinoids have a remarkable safety record, particularly when compared to other therapeutically active substances."

Medical marijuana has numerous medical benefits, argues Paul Armentano in the following viewpoint. He presents the results of various studies that have concluded that marijuana is a first-rate treatment for multiple diseases and disorders. Armentano contends that marijuana has been more thoroughly tested for safety and efficacy than most synthetic drugs, so Americans can be reasonably sure that it is safe, effective, and truly medicinal. Armentano says researchers are continually learning new ways marijuana can treat or relieve disease, and thus concludes that the benefits of using marijuana with a doctor's supervision outweigh the risks.

Armentano is deputy director of the National Organization for the Reform of Marijuana Laws.

AS YOU READ, CONSIDER THE FOLLOWING QUESTIONS:
1. What did the University of California Center for Medicinal Cannabis Research find about smoked marijuana's ability to alleviate neuropathic pain, according to Armentano?
2. How many scientific papers does Armentano say have been published that analyze marijuana?
3. What did the American Medical Association conclude in 2009, according to the author?

D espite the ongoing political debate regarding the legality of medical marijuana, clinical investigations of the therapeutic use of cannabinoids are now more prevalent than at any time in history.

A Heavily Studied First-Rate Treatment

For example, in February 2010 investigators at the University of California Center for Medicinal Cannabis Research publicly announced the findings of a series of randomized, placebo-controlled clinical trials on the medical utility of inhaled cannabis. The studies, which utilized the so-called "gold standard" FDA [US Food and Drug Administration] clinical trial design, concluded that marijuana ought to be a "first line treatment" for patients with neuropathy and other serious illnesses.

Among the studies conducted by the Center, four assessed smoked marijuana's ability to alleviate neuropathic pain, a notoriously difficult to treat type of nerve pain associated with cancer, diabetes, HIV/AIDS, spinal cord injury and many other debilitating conditions. Each of the trials found that cannabis consistently reduced patients' pain levels to a degree that was as good or better than currently available medications.

Another study conducted by the Center's investigators assessed the use of marijuana as a treatment for patients suffering from multiple sclerosis [MS]. That study determined that "smoked cannabis was superior to placebo in reducing spasticity and pain in patients with MS, and provided some benefit beyond currently prescribed treatments."

Around the globe, similarly controlled trials are also taking place. A 2010 review by researchers in Germany reports that since 2005 there have been 37 controlled studies assessing the safety and efficacy of marijuana and its naturally occurring compounds in a total of 2,563

In the foreground is a copy of the report on medical marijuana benefits conducted by the University of California Center for Medicinal Cannabis Research. The report, released in 2010, concluded that marijuana is an effective treatment for a number of serious illnesses.

subjects. By contrast, most FDA-approved drugs go through far fewer trials involving far fewer subjects.

A Growing Body of Research

While much of the renewed interest in cannabinoid therapeutics is a result of the discovery of the endocannabinoid regulatory system some of this increased attention is also due to the growing body of testimonials from medical cannabis patients and their physicians. Nevertheless, despite this influx of anecdotal reports, much of the modern investigation of medical cannabis remains limited to preclinical (animal) studies of individual cannabinoids (e.g. THC or cannabidiol) and/or synthetic cannabinoid agonists (e.g., dronabinol or WIN 55,212-2) rather than clinical trial investigations involving whole plant material. Because of the US government's strong public policy stance against any use of cannabis, the bulk of this modern cannabinoid research is predictably taking place outside the United States.

As clinical research into the therapeutic value of cannabinoids has proliferated—there are now an estimated 20,000 published papers in the scientific literature analyzing marijuana and its constituents—so too has investigators' understanding of cannabis' remarkable capability to combat disease. Whereas researchers in the 1970s, 80s, and 90s primarily assessed cannabis' ability to temporarily alleviate various disease symptoms—such as the nausea associated with cancer chemotherapy—scientists today are exploring the potential role of cannabinoids to modify disease.

Of particular interest, scientists are investigating cannabinoids' capacity to moderate autoimmune disorders such as multiple sclerosis, rheumatoid arthritis, and inflammatory bowel disease, as well as their role in the treatment of neurological disorders such as Alzheimer's disease and amyotrophic lateral sclerosis (a.k.a. Lou Gehrig's disease.) In fact, in 2009, the American Medical Association (AMA) resolved for the first time in the organization's history "that marijuana's status as a federal Schedule I controlled substance be reviewed with the goal of facilitating the conduct of clinical research and development of cannabinoid-based medicines."

Investigators are also studying the anti-cancer activities of cannabis, as a growing body of preclinical and clinical data concludes that cannabinoids can reduce the spread of specific cancer cells via apoptosis (programmed cell death) and by the inhibition of angiogenesis (the formation of new blood vessels). Arguably, these latter findings represent far broader and more significant applications for cannabinoid therapeutics than researchers could have imagined some thirty or even twenty years ago.

A Remarkable Safety Record

Cannabinoids have a remarkable safety record, particularly when compared to other therapeutically active substances. Most significantly, the consumption of marijuana—regardless of quantity or potency—cannot induce a fatal overdose. According to a 1995 review prepared for the World Health Organization, "There are no recorded cases of overdose fatalities attributed to cannabis, and the estimated lethal dose for humans extrapolated from animal studies is so high that it cannot be achieved by . . . users."

In 2008, investigators at McGill University Health Centre and McGill University in Montreal and the University of British Columbia in Vancouver reviewed 23 clinical investigations of medical cannabinoid drugs (typically oral THC or liquid cannabis extracts) and eight observational studies conducted between 1966 and 2007. Investigators "did not find a higher incidence rate of serious adverse events associated with medical cannabinoid use" compared to non-using controls over these four decades.

That said, cannabis should not necessarily be viewed as a "harmless" substance. Its active constituents may produce a variety of physiological and euphoric effects.

> **FAST FACT**
>
> A 2010 Gallup poll found that 70 percent of Americans favored making marijuana legally available for doctors to prescribe in order to reduce patients' pain and suffering.

As a result, there may be some populations that are susceptible to increased risks from the use of cannabis, such as adolescents, pregnant or nursing mothers, and patients who have a family history of mental illness.

Patients with hepatitis C, decreased lung function (such as chronic obstructive pulmonary disease), or who have a history of heart disease or stroke may also be at a greater risk of experiencing adverse side effects from marijuana. As with any medication, patients should consult thoroughly with their physician before deciding whether the medical use of cannabis is safe and appropriate.

Marijuana Can Treat Numerous Diseases

As states continue to approve legislation enabling the physician-supervised use of medical marijuana, more patients with varying disease types are exploring the use of therapeutic cannabis. Many of these patients and their physicians are now discussing this issue for the first time and are seeking guidance on whether the therapeutic use of cannabis may or may not be advisable. . . . [There is] recently published scientific research (2000–2010) on the therapeutic use of cannabis and cannabinoids for 19 clinical indications:

- Alzheimer's disease
- Amyotrophic lateral sclerosis
- Chronic pain
- Diabetes mellitus
- Dystonia
- Fibromyalgia
- Gastrointestinal disorders
- Gliomas/other cancers
- Hepatitis C
- Human immunodeficiency virus
- Hypertension
- Incontinence
- Methicillin-resistant *Staphyloccus aureus* (MRSA)
- Multiple sclerosis
- Osteoporosis
- Pruritus
- Rheumatoid arthritis
- Sleep apnea
- Tourette's syndrome

Americans Approve of Medical Marijuana

A 2010 poll asked Americans if they approved of marijuana legalization for any purpose, for personal use, or for medical reasons. Even when they opposed legalization of marijuana for any purpose or for personal use, Americans approved of legalizing marijuana for medical purposes.

Question: "Do you favor, oppose, or neither favor nor oppose the complete legalization of the use of marijuana for any purpose?"

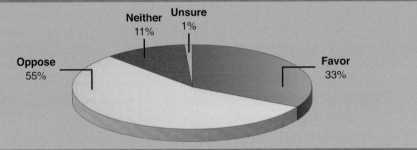

Neither 11%
Unsure 1%
Oppose 55%
Favor 33%

Question: "Do you favor, oppose, or neither favor nor oppose legalizing the possession of small amounts of marijuana for personal use?"

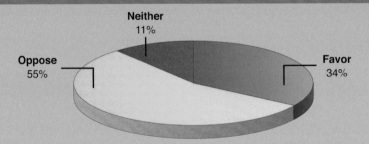

Neither 11%
Oppose 55%
Favor 34%

Question: "Do you favor, oppose, or neither favor nor oppose legalizing the possession of small amounts of marijuana for medical purposes?"

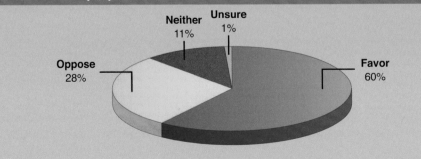

Neither 11%
Unsure 1%
Oppose 28%
Favor 60%

Adapted from: AP-CNBC poll conducted by GfK Roper Public Affairs & Media, April 7–12, 2010.

In some of these cases, modern science is now affirming longtime anecdotal reports of medical cannabis users (e.g., the use of cannabis to alleviate GI [gastrointestinal] disorders). In other cases, this research is highlighting entirely new potential clinical utilities for cannabinoids (e.g., the use of cannabinoids to modify the progression of diabetes.)

EVALUATING THE AUTHOR'S ARGUMENTS:

Paul Armentano argues that marijuana, when used correctly, is a safe and effective medicine. Mehmet Oz and Mike Roizen, authors of the previous viewpoint, disagree. After reading both viewpoints, with which position do you ultimately agree? Why? List at least two pieces of evidence that swayed you.

Spice and Other Legal Forms of Synthetic Marijuana Should Be Banned

"Spice and other so-called 'synthetic cannabinoids' escape existing drugs laws because they do not contain marijuana and are not chemically related to it."

Independent

The following viewpoint was originally published in the *Independent,* a British newspaper providing worldwide breaking news. The newspaper reports that British officials are saying that Spice, a synthetic form of marijuana, is more dangerous than natural marijuana. The officials argue that Spice is made from dangerous chemicals and can cause paranoia and panic attacks, and even heart problems. For these reasons—and because the chemicals in the drug are often different from those advertised, and the quantities of chemicals are unknown to the user—British officials say synthetic forms of marijuana like Spice may pose a significant health risk and should be banned.

1. What are Spice and other "synthetic cannabinoids" legally sold as?
2. According to the viewpoint, why is synthetic marijuana potentially more dangerous than natural marijuana?
3. How much does Spice cost when compared with cannabis, as reported in the viewpoint?

A "herbal high" that mimics the effect of cannabis should be banned, the Government's drug adviser said today.

The Advisory Council on the Misuse of Drugs said Spice could be more powerful than cannabis.

Pouches of the drug are widely available on the Internet and in so-called "head shops" for around £20.

> ## FAST FACT
>
> A ban on Spice and other synthetic marijuana products went into effect in Wisconsin in July 2011. The penalty for possessing the drug was up to six months in prison, while distributing the product was punishable by up to forty years.

Spice Is Dangerous

The council's chairman, Professor David Nutt, said although it was sold as a "natural" high, Spice was created using dangerous chemicals.

He said: "Spice and other synthetic cannabinoid products are being sold legally as harmless 'herbal legal highs'.

"However, the herbal content is coated in one or more dangerous chemical compounds that mimic the effects of cannabis.

"These are not harmless herbal alternatives and have been found to cause paranoia and panic attacks.

"That is why we are advising the Government to bring a large number of synthetic cannabinoids under the Misuse of Drugs Act."

Spice and other so-called "synthetic cannabinoids" escape existing drugs laws because they do not contain marijuana and are not chemically related to it.

But by spraying synthetic additives on to herbs, dealers can create similar intoxication in users to that caused by THC, the active ingredient in cannabis.

Spice Could Be More Harmful than Marijuana

Analysis of samples of Spice show it has a "higher potency" than THC, the Advisory Council on the Misuse of Drugs (ACMD) warned.

It said Spice could be "more harmful" because the quantity of chemicals in the drug is "unknown to the user".

Home Secretary Alan Johnson is expected to legislate later this year [2009] to ban Spice. It is likely to be made a class B drug, alongside cannabis.

A Home Office spokesman said: "We are determined to crack down on those so-called 'legal highs' that pose a significant health risk.

"To this end, earlier this year we asked the ACMD to look into the harms caused by so called 'legal highs' and recently received its advice on this group of man-made chemicals that act on the body in a similar way to cannabis.

"These have been recently found in herbal smoking products, including products sold under the brand name 'Spice'.

Also called K2, Spice—a synthetic form of marijuana touted as providing a "natural" high—is actually loaded with dangerous chemicals, according to government experts.

States Move to Ban Synthetic Marijuana

As of May 2011, at least 18 states had banned synthetic marijuana, or "Spice," and more than a dozen states were considering a ban. Numerous townships, counties, and cities have also banned the substance.

States that have banned synthetic marijuana

States considering a ban on synthetic marijuana

[Compiled from various sources by the Editor.]

"We will publish our response shortly, along with the proposed controls for a range of other substances.

"We remain committed to tackling drug use in all its forms through tough enforcement, education and, where required, treatment. And it remains important that we continue to adapt our drug policy to tackle the changing environment in order to protect the public, especially our young people, from drug harms."

Spice Remains Legal for Now

The review of legal highs was requested by former home secretary Jacqui Smith earlier this year and follows moves to ban Spice in Germany, Austria and France.

At around £20 for three grams of Spice—sold under brands such as Spice Silver, Spice Gold, Spice Diamond and Spice Yucatan Fire—prices are similar to cannabis.

The ACMD's report said herbs listed on the packets of the drug were often not found inside, but they did discover large amounts of Vitamin E used to hide other chemicals.

The council admitted there is little detailed information about the size of the Spice market but it is clearly "extensive" and distribution networks [are] "well developed".

Reports from Germany suggested some users suffered heart problems after smoking the drug.

The ACMD's report stated: "Users cannot . . . assume the same effects from the same product the next time they use it.

"Thus, there is potential for overdose should a person use a particularly strong batch or a synthetic cannabinoid with particularly high potency."

EVALUATING THE AUTHOR'S ARGUMENTS:

The *Independent* reports that British authorities say that Spice should be banned. Explain your own views concerning the drug's prohibition. Should it be banned? Should there be an age minimum to buy it? Should its use be legal? Then, make a recommendation for how lawmakers should deal with Spice.

Viewpoint

6

Bans on Legal Forms of Synthetic Marijuana Are Ineffective

Alan Scher Zagier

"Business is just as good, if not better, since Missouri's [synthetic marijuana] ban took effect."

In the following viewpoint Alan Scher Zagier reports that laws prohibiting the sale of synthetic marijuana have proven ineffective. When one type of synthetic marijuana is banned, distributors are quick to develop a new kind and sell that instead. Zagier reports that bans have even encouraged distributors to create new kinds of products. In addition, he says, bans have merely pushed business underground, away from the eyes of law enforcement. Most of all, bans have not stopped customers from wanting synthetic marijuana, Zagier claims, and where there is market demand, the market will provide. For all of these reasons it seems unlikely that banning synthetic marijuana will be effective, the author claims.

Zagier is a reporter for the Associated Press.

AS YOU READ, CONSIDER THE FOLLOWING QUESTIONS:
  1. What are K2 and K3, and what do they lend to Zagier's argument?
  2. Who is John Huffman and how does he factor into the author's report?
  3. Who is Micah Riggs? What does his story lend to the viewpoint?

A uthorities in 13 states thought they were acting to curb a public health threat when they outlawed a form of synthetic marijuana known as K2, a concoction of dried herbs sprayed with chemicals.

But before the laws took effect, many stores that did a brisk business in fake pot had already gotten around the bans by making slight changes to K2's chemical formula, creating knockoffs with names such as "K3," "Heaven Scent" and "Syn."

"It's kind of pointless," said University of Missouri sophomore Brittany May after purchasing a K2 alternative called "BoCoMo Dew" at a Columbia smoke shop. "They're just going to come up with another thing."

Meaningless Laws

Barely six months after Kansas adopted the nation's first ban on K2, even police acknowledge that the laws are all but meaningless because merchants can so easily offer legal alternatives.

Until a year ago, products such as K2 were virtually unknown in the United States. Clemson University chemistry professor John Huffman developed the compounds in 1995 while researching the effect of cannabinoids, the active compounds found in marijuana.

Mr. Huffman had little reason to think his lab work would morph into a commercial product. He calls users of K2 and its chemical cousins "idiots," noting the lack of research into the substance's effects, which include reports of rapid heartbeats and high blood pressure. It's often labeled as incense with warnings against human consumption.

Yet Mr. Huffman has little faith that the bans designed to combat the problem will deter manufacturers or consumers. "It's not going to be effective," he said. "Is the ban on marijuana effective?"

Banning Drugs Does Not Eradicate Their Use

An unscientific poll taken by Midlands Connect, the Fox News affiliate that serves Columbia, South Carolina, found that most viewers thought synthetic marijuana should not be banned.

Question: "What do you think about legal synthetic marijuana developed by a Clemson University professor that is now for sale across South Carolina?"

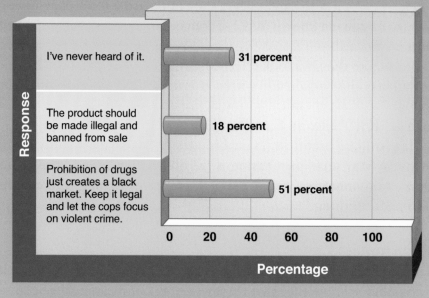

Taken from: MidlandsConnect.com/WACH-TV (Fox News affiliate, Columbia, SC), May 4, 2011.

Law Enforcement Will Not Be Effective

He also doubts that law enforcement agencies will be able to devote the necessary resources to identify such complex creations as "1-pentyl-3-(1-naphthoyl)indole," the substance's scientific name. The compound sold as K2 is also known by the scientific shorthand of JWH-018, a nod to its creator's initials.

"The guy in the average crime lab isn't really capable of doing the kind of sophisticated tests necessary" to identify the substance, he said.

The bans were adopted by lawmakers or public health officials in Alabama, Arkansas, Georgia, Hawaii, Iowa, Illinois, Kansas,

Kentucky, Louisiana, Mississippi, Missouri, North Dakota and Tennessee.

Missouri state Sen. Kurt Schaefer, a Republican from Columbia, acknowledges that the marketplace has quickly adapted to his state's ban. He also thinks that the new law, along with a wave of media reports, is an effective deterrent, especially for potential users under 18, and their parents.

"We've at least minimized the threat to public safety," he said.

The Missouri statute identifies five synthetic cannabinoids by name, but leaves out many others.

Police and public health experts say that users seeking the more benign high associated with marijuana may be unprepared for the synthetic version. Users of K2 describe a more intense but shorter high, with effects lasting about 20 minutes as opposed to several hours.

Mr. Schaefer said lawmakers may consider a broader ban next year if the law proves ineffective. He also drew a sharp distinction between synthetic marijuana and the natural alternative.

"No one should confuse this product with marijuana," he said. "This is guys standing around in a factory wearing rubber boots and spraying chemicals on dried leaves."

Bans Have Not Stopped Sales

The state bans were enacted starting in March [2010]. Similar proposals are pending in New York, Ohio, Indiana, Michigan, New Jersey and Pennsylvania. And many local governments have enacted their own prohibitions.

But new laws have not prevented a seemingly brisk online business. The website K2Fast.com, for instance, touts its ability to "ship fast to any state" while noting its product does not contain JWH-018, the ingredient that was just made illegal.

Mississippi legislators examine a vial of Spice (synthetic marijuana). Critics say that bans of the substance will simply cause distributors to develop new versions of the drug.

Alternatives are widely available in head shops, gas stations, convenience stores and coffee houses.

Micah Riggs, owner of the Coffee Wonk in Kansas City, said his business is just as good, if not better, since Missouri's ban took effect. He says his newest blend is stronger and has a smoother taste than the banned form of K2. It's been so successful that Mr. Riggs is considering expanding his operations to Florida and New York.

"I researched this stuff pretty heavily before I started selling it," he said. "I'm not just going to take a risk with people's health."

Bans Push Business Underground

The Georgia Poison Control Center has seen just a "trickling" of K2 cases since legislators outlawed the product in May, said Gaylord Lopez, the center's director.

Mr. Lopez, who visited several Atlanta stores that continue to sell K2, said he was not aware of an increase in knockoff products since the ban was enacted. He said the trade in K2 has just "gone underground" now that it's illegal.

"If you play the part, and don't look like a DEA [Drug Enforcement Administration] agent, they tell you they still have it," he said.

In Columbia, a smoke shop called BoCoMo Bay saw a surge of interest in K2 and its legal alternatives around the time legislators began discussing a ban.

Owner Kevin Bay said his loyal customers include factory workers, computer technicians, even soccer moms. The substance is also popular with people who must submit to drug tests, such as firefighters, police officers and people on probation.

Bans Promote Innovation

Mr. Bay estimates that he sells an average of 80 bags a day of the various blends, which cost $25 for three grams—similar to the street price for low-end marijuana. Demand is so high, it takes four employees working four-hour shifts, three days a week, to package the 2.2-pound bulk shipments into smaller servings.

Mr. Bay, who testified against the K2 ban at the Capitol in Jefferson City, calls the effort to ban the substance another losing battle in the war on drugs. If lawmakers adopt a broader law, that will just promote more innovation in the laboratory, he predicts.

"You can't prohibit something that hasn't been invented yet," he said.

> **EVALUATING THE AUTHOR'S ARGUMENTS:**
>
> Alan Scher Zagier quotes from several sources to support the points he makes in his essay. Make a list of everyone he quotes, including their credentials and the nature of their comments. Then, analyze his sources—are they credible? Are they well qualified to speak on this subject? What specific points do they support?

Chapter 3

How Should Society Respond to Drug Abuse?

Bundles of cocaine confiscated by the US Coast Guard are stacked on a California dock.

The War on Drugs Has Been Successful

Michele M. Leonhart

"DEA's operational successes and strong partnerships are resulting in measurable impacts on the domestic illicit drug market."

In the following viewpoint Michele M. Leonhart argues that the United States is winning the war on drugs. She reviews key successes in the drug war that have resulted in thousands of arrests and the seizure of millions of dollars and tons of drugs and weapons. The Drug Enforcement Administration's (DEA's) successful operations have caused drugs to become weaker and less affordable, which Leonhart argues drives down demand for drugs among the population. Leonhart points to statistics that show a decline in teen drug use as proof that the United States is winning the war on drugs.

From 2007 to 2010 Leonhart served as the acting administrator of the DEA. In 2010 she was nominated for the position of and confirmed as administrator of the DEA, a wing of the US Department of Justice charged with combating illegal drug trafficking and use. This viewpoint contains her testimony (during her time as acting administrator) before the US House Subcommittee on Commerce, Justice, Science, and Related Industries.

Michele M. Leonhart, Statement to the House Subcommittee on Commerce, Justice, Science, and Related Agencies, www.justice.gov, March 26, 2009.

AS YOU READ, CONSIDER THE FOLLOWING QUESTIONS:
1. What is Operation Xcellerator and how does it factor into the author's argument?
2. How many people were arrested in Project Reckoning, according to Leonhart? How many tons of cocaine and pounds of marijuana were seized?
3. By how much does Leonhart say the price of cocaine changed from January 2007 to December 2008?

D EA's [Drug Enforcement Administration's] mission is to enforce the controlled substances laws and regulations of the United States. To this end, DEA Special Agents, Intelligence Analysts, and Diversion Investigators build cases that target the individuals and organizations involved in growing, manufacturing, and distributing controlled substances appearing in or destined for illicit traffic in the United States. DEA's accomplishments over the past year are many. For the sake of time, I will highlight just a few of them.

Several Major Victories in the War on Drugs

DEA achieved several major victories against the Mexican drug cartels this year [2009].

For example, in February 2009, DEA concluded Operation Xcellerator, a 21-month multi-agency investigation targeting the Sinaloa Cartel. The Sinaloa Cartel dominates much of the drug smuggling on the Southwest Border and is responsible for bringing multi-ton quantities of cocaine and marijuana from Mexico into the United States through an enterprise of distribution cells in the United States and Canada. Furthermore, the Sinaloa Cartel is responsible for laundering hundreds of millions of dollars in criminal proceeds from illegal drug trafficking activities. As of February 25, 2009, Operation Xcellerator has led to the arrest of 781 individuals and the seizure of approximately $61 million in U.S. currency and $10 million in drug related assets. Additional seizures include more than 12.5 metric tons of cocaine, more than 8 metric tons of marijuana, more than 1,200 pounds of methamphetamine, approximately 1.5 million pills of Ecstasy, and 191 weapons. As DEA's most focused attack against the Sinaloa Cartel to date, Operation Xcellerator demonstrates DEA's relentless efforts to disrupt and dismantle major drug cartels.

Project Reckoning is an ongoing multi-operational initiative targeting the Gulf Cartel. The Gulf Cartel and its former enforcement arm, known as the Zetas, are responsible for a large proportion of the drug-related violence in Mexico and, like the rival Sinaloa Cartel, are responsible for bringing multi-ton quantities of cocaine and marijuana from Mexico into the United States. To date, Project Reckoning has led to the arrest of 632 individuals, the indictment of the entire upper echelon of the Gulf Cartel, including Jaime Gonzalez Duran, aka "Hummer," and the seizure of over $71.8 million in U.S. currency, with an additional $17 million in other assets seized. Drug

Drug Enforcement Administration officials display cash and drugs seized in a Project Reckoning operation against a Mexican drug cartel.

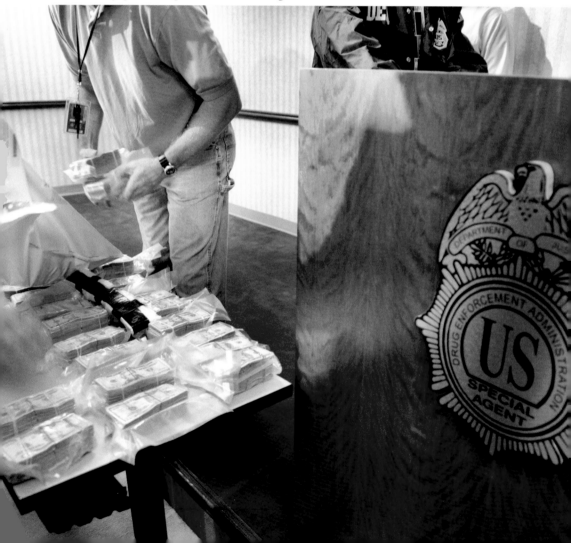

seizures include more than 17 metric tons of cocaine, more than 64,000 pounds of marijuana, more than 1,300 pounds of methamphetamine and 19 kilograms of heroin. Two hundred and twenty-five weapons were also seized, which included explosive devices and weapons capable of fully automatic fire. Additionally, approximately two days prior to his arrest, a personal weapons cache belonging to Duran was seized in Mexico in November 2008. The cache consisted of 540 assault rifles, more than 500,000 rounds of ammunition, 150 grenades, 14 cartridges of dynamite, 98 fragmentation grenades, 67 bulletproof vests, seven Barrett .50-caliber sniper rifles, and a Light Anti-Tank rocket. . . .

FAST FACT

The Drug Enforcement Administration counts among its successes the fact that in 2009, 21 percent fewer teenagers had used illicit drugs than in the decade prior.

Attacks and Arrests

Operation All Inclusive (OAI) is the primary DFAS [Drug Flow Attack Strategy] enforcement operation in the Western Hemisphere transit zones. OAI is a combination of sequential and simultaneous land, air, maritime, and financial attacks, guided by intelligence and synchronized with other agencies to disrupt the illicit trafficking patterns and the drug trafficking organizations themselves. Iterations of OAI have been staged annually since 2005, and the results have been significant.

OAI 2008 ran from January 15 to October 20, 2008, and involved DEA, the Joint Interagency Task Force–South, Customs and Border Protection, the U.S. Coast Guard, the Defense Intelligence Agency, the Central Intelligence Agency's Crime and Narcotics Center, the National Geospatial Intelligence Agency, the National Security Agency, the Office of Naval Intelligence, and a number of host nation counterparts. OAI 2008 focused on disrupting the flow of drugs, chemicals and money from the source zone in South America, through the transit zone of Mexico, Central America, and the Caribbean, and into the United States. This iteration of OAI expanded the geographical coverage to include portions of the Southwest Border and the Andean Region, including Peru, Brazil and Bolivia.

Drug Movement Into and Within the United States

The majority of illegal drugs come into the United States via land smuggling (versus drugs smuggled on boats or planes). Drug trafficking is heavier along the southern border with Mexico, though drugs enter from the north, via Canada, too.

Northern Border Seizures

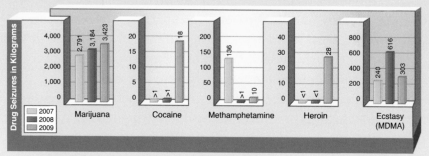

Southern Border Seizures

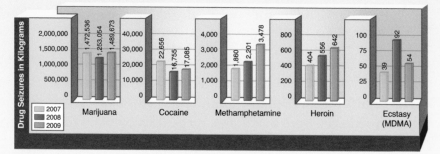

Taken from: US Department of Justice, National Drug Intelligence Center, *National Drug Threat Assessment 2010*, February 2010.

The overwhelming success of OAI 2008 can be measured by the seizure of 100 metric tons of cocaine; the seizure of more than $92 million in U.S. currency/assets; and the arrest of Consolidated Priority Organization Targets Jorge Mario Paredes-Cordova and Eduardo Arellano-Felix, and Priority Targets Luis Urbina-Amaya, Lester Marina-Pastor, and Juan Rivera-Perez. Additional highlights include the seizure of an underground weapons training facility in Tijuana, Mexico controlled by the Arellano-Felix drug trafficking organization; a single seizure of almost $12 million in U.S. currency from a containerized cargo shipment seized at the Port of Manzanillo, Colima, Mexico; and the first-ever seizure by the Mexican Navy of a self-propelled semi-submersible smuggling vessel off the Pacific Coast of Mexico. From this vessel, a total of 5.8 metric tons of cocaine was seized and four Colombian nationals were arrested. . . .

DEA's operational successes and strong partnerships are resulting in measurable impacts on the domestic illicit drug market and quantifiable results in terms of revenue denied and asset seizures.

Drugs Are Weaker and Less Affordable

According to DEA's analysis of cocaine seizures, the price of cocaine in the United States has risen significantly over the past two years, while purity of the drug has decreased. From January 2007 to December 2008, the price per pure gram of cocaine has increased 104.5 percent, from $97.62 to $199.60, while purity decreased 34.8 percent, from 67.2 to 43.9 percent purity. Factors contributing to these favorable results include, but are not limited to:

- DEA's Drug Flow Attack Strategy
- DEA-led operations such as Operation All Inclusive
- Extraditions from Mexico and Colombia
- Building coalitions with host nation counterparts
- More than $9 billion of revenue denied to drug traffickers from FY 2005 though FY 2008
- Combined efforts of DEA and its Federal, State, and local law enforcement partners.

The results for methamphetamine price and purity, while not as impressive as they were a year ago, are still favorable. From January 2007 to December 2008, the price per pure gram of methamphetamine increased 20.4 percent, from $148.03 to $178.30 while the purity increased slightly from 56.9 percent to 59.9 percent purity. However, at the end of 2007, the price per pure gram of methamphetamine was $267.74 while the purity was 40.9 percent. Much of the methamphetamine trend that was observed at this time last year could be attributed to the success of our enforcement efforts, state legislation and the Combat Methamphetamine Epidemic Act (CMEA), which made it difficult for producers of domestic methamphetamine to obtain the needed precursor chemicals. The partial reversal of this trend in the past 12 months is a result of drug traffickers adapting to the CMEA and changing their production and trafficking patterns. Small toxic lab seizures in the U.S. are beginning to rise again as the traffickers adapt to various forms of legislation. Domestic production is now being fueled by varying forms of "smurfing," numerous individuals going from store to store purchasing the maximum limit at each store and then pooling their purchases. Additionally, Mexican drug trafficking organizations are producing and distributing much of the methamphetamine consumed in our country. DEA is adapting to this production shift as we focus on methamphetamine produced in Mexico and transported across the Southwest Border. . . .

Decline in Teen Drug Use Is Proof We Are Winning

Switching briefly to a discussion of drug use in America, I am happy to report that illicit drug use by American teens continues to decline. According to the 2008 Monitoring the Future Survey, current illicit drug use among 8th, 10th, and 12th graders declined by 25 percent from 2001 to 2008, meaning there were approximately 900,000 fewer teens using drugs in 2008 than in 2001. Most notably, methamphetamine use among high school seniors dropped from 2.5 percent in 2005 to 1.2 percent in 2008 and cocaine use among high school seniors decreased from 5.1 percent in 2005 to 4.4 percent in 2008. In addition, drug use among workers is at its lowest level in 19 years. Since 1988, positive workplace drug tests have fallen by 72 percent, from 13.6 percent in 1988 to 3.8 percent in 2007. DEA is proud to be a key partner in reducing drug abuse in America by reducing the supply of drugs that are available. Effective drug prevention and treatment programs are less likely to succeed if Americans are surrounded by cheap and plentiful drugs.

EVALUATING THE AUTHOR'S ARGUMENTS:

To make her argument Michele M. Leonhart points to thousands of arrests, tons of drugs, and millions of dollars that have been seized in multiple antidrug operations. In her opinion, these are proof that the war on drugs has been successful. How might Sara Miller Llana, author of the following viewpoint, interpret these arrests and seizures? Write two to three sentences on how you think she might respond to Leonhart's assertion that the war on drugs has been successful. Then, state with which author you agree.

The War on Drugs Is a Failure

Sara Miller Llana

"The global war on drugs has failed, with devastating consequences for individuals and societies around the world."

In the following viewpoint Sara Miller Llana reports on the findings of a report by the Global Commission on Drug Policy. The report suggests that the war on drugs is a failure and cannot be won, as violence and drug use have increased rather than diminished. The commission is not saying anything new; however, the impressive credentials of its members add weight to its recommendations. Commission members include a former UN secretary-general, a former US secretary of state, a former Federal Reserve chief, and the former presidents of Mexico, Switzerland, Brazil, and a billionaire. The commission urges countries to combat violent organized crime, to help nonviolent drug users, and to regulate currently illegal drugs as part of the legal drug market.

Llana is a staff writer for the *Christian Science Monitor,* a national newspaper.

1. Why, according to Llana, has it become harder to keep track of the various players in the "war on drugs"?
2. What, according to the viewpoint, is recommended as an alternative to incarceration for drug users?
3. How did the United States address the report released by the Global Commission on Drug Policy, according to the author?

I t used to be easier to keep track of the various players in the "war on drugs."

There were "northern" consumers and "southern" producers and smugglers.

But now the roles are beginning to merge. The US is still the biggest market for illegal drugs, but drug use across the Americas is up. An overwhelming portion of the violence is in Mexico, but it is getting uncomfortably close to the US doorstep.

The Drug War Has Failed

The picture of a drug war that's witnessed the simultaneous geographic spread of violence and use is at the heart of a report released Thursday [June 2, 2011] by the Global Commission on Drug Policy that urges experiments with legalization and regulation as a way to reduce violence. "The global war on drugs has failed, with devastating consequences for individuals and societies around the world," the report states.

The argument that criminalization has failed isn't new. But the names backing the report go far beyond the drug reform "usual suspects." Among the 19 members of the commission are former UN Secretary General Kofi Annan, former Secretary of State George Shultz, former Federal Reserve chief Paul Volcker, former Mexican President Ernesto Zedillo, former Swiss President Ruth Dreifuss, former Brazilian President Fernando Henrique Cardoso, and billionaire Richard Branson.

"They are not saying anything new," says Jorge Hernández Tinajero, the president of Cuphid, a group in Mexico that disseminates information about drug policies. "But the people are new. These are powerful people."

"Not the usual suspects," agrees Adam Isacson, a senior associate at the Washington Office on Latin America and expert on US drug policy.

Helping Hand

The commission recommends that countries help, rather than incarcerate, drug users who do not hurt others and focus on punishing violent organized crime instead. "Political leaders and public figures should have the courage to articulate publicly what many of them acknowledge privately: that the evidence overwhelmingly demonstrates that repressive strategies will not solve the drug problem, and that the war on drugs has not, and cannot, be won," their report says. . . .

It urges governments to experiment with regulating a legal drug market, and points to successes in Europe, such as Portugal, to make its case.

The report builds on work by a Latin American commission in 2009 headed by the former presidents from Mexico, Brazil, and Colombia, which also concluded that the "war on drugs" had failed, as has prohibition.

> ## FAST FACT
>
> Two weeks before the fortieth anniversary of the war on drugs (in June 2011), the Global Commission on Drug Policy reported that between 1998 and 2008 the global consumption of opiates increased 34.5 percent, cocaine 27 percent, and marijuana 8.5 percent.

The US dismissed the report. "The bottom line is that balanced drug control efforts are making a big difference," Rafael Lemaitre, communications director of the White House Office of National Drug Control Policy, said in a statement.

Growing Problems with Drug Use

Many in Latin America have long faulted the US government for not paying enough attention to drug consumption, instead focusing on the security side of the issue. Now such countries are starting to deal with their own scourge of drug use. "The dichotomy is false . . . There is growth in the use of both cocaine and heroin in the so-called

Funding for the War on Drugs

Each year the United States spends thousands of millions of dollars on different aspects of the drug war. Opponents say the war on drugs is too costly.

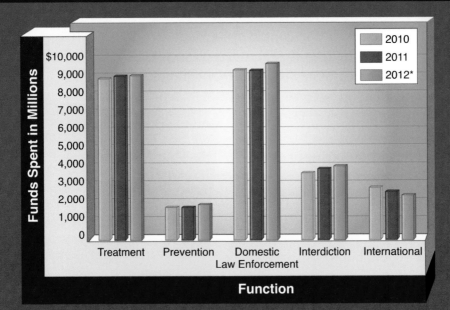

*Funds requested

Total Funds Spent and Requested in Millions

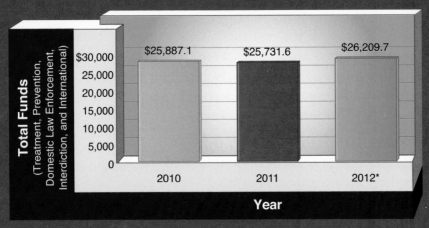

*Funds requested

Taken from: Office of National Drug Control Policy, *National Drug Control Strategy: FY 2012 Budget and Performance Summary*, April 2011, p. 19.

developing world," says Bruce Bagley, a drug-trafficking expert at the University of Miami.

In that way, leaders from traditional consuming and producing countries are getting on the same page in certain respects, underlined by the commission report signed by leaders from across the globe. Mr. Bagley supports the report as another message in changing the paradigm, but he says it has a "middle class" focus that fails to provide alternatives for coca producers in Bolivia or poppy growers in Afghanistan who also play a critical role in the chain.

EVALUATING THE AUTHOR'S ARGUMENTS:

Sara Miller Llana reports on the Global Commission of Drug Policy's recommendation that countries help, rather than incarcerate, nonviolent drug offenders. Think about what you would recommend to help drug users. What do you think would help drug addicts become, and stay, clean?

Drug Addicts Should Be Locked Up in Rehab

"Take these addicts and lock them up until they're clean. Make them stop breaking into our cars, breaking into our homes. Make them stop visiting the emergency room dozens of times a year."

Ethan Baron

In the following viewpoint Ethan Baron argues that drug addicts should be locked up until they are clean and sober. In his opinion, letting addicts roam the streets puts them and others at risk, increases crime, brings down property values, and perpetuates the cycle of drug addiction. He says it makes more sense, and would be more cost-effective overall, to force addicts to enter long-term drug treatment programs. Baron argues that locking up addicts would not violate their civil liberties. In his opinion, addicts forfeited their rights when they decided to steal from society and break the law. He concludes that cities perpetuate their drug problem when they refuse to take strong action toward addicts.

Baron is a columnist for *The Province*, the Canadian publication in British Columbia that originally published this viewpoint.

AS YOU READ, CONSIDER THE FOLLOWING QUESTIONS:

1. Who are Brenda Burridge and Claire Addey-Jibb and how do they factor into Baron's argument?
2. What are two reasons Baron says drug addicts cannot be trusted to make rational decisions for themselves?
3. What, according to the author, does society have a moral duty to do for drug addicts?

There is no logic here.

Those are the words of Vancouver police Const. Brenda Burridge, talking about the Downtown Eastside, her beat for the past six years.

Those five words say it all.

Where is the logic in thousands of people taking drugs that turn their lives into a miserable shuffle toward death?

Where is the logic in warehousing addicts in a neighbourhood where drugs are sold on every block?

Where is the logic in letting these addicts suck tens of millions of dollars a year out of our taxes and personal property while the government does virtually nothing to treat their addictions?

Where is the logic in funding hundreds of social agencies whose primary purpose is supporting people who are locked into drug dependency?

On a recent visit to the Downtown Eastside, I spent two hours walking the beat with Burridge and Const. Claire Addey-Jibb, who spent a great deal of time searching addicts who were huddled in doorways and alleys, smoking and injecting crack and cocaine and shooting heroin.

"Pull your pants up, gather your things up and go back to your room," Burridge told one man after he scattered his tiny amount of cocaine when caught preparing to inject it in a Blood Alley court-yard.

Here's some logic: Take these addicts and lock them up until they're clean.

Make them stop breaking into our cars, breaking into our homes. Make them stop visiting the emergency room dozens of times a year.

Make them stop turning downtown Vancouver into a showcase of urban blight.

Make them become the people they could have been had they not become drug addicts.

These people, in the grip of their addictions, cannot be responsible for making decisions for themselves.

They need to be forced into long-term drug treatment.

The author contends that because drug addicts in the vise of addiction cannot make responsible personal decisions, they should be forced into long-term treatment.

There are those who say that if an addict doesn't want to quit, rehabilitation will fail. But an addict who is busy feeding his addiction is not the person to decide whether he should get drug treatment. He needs to be locked up and detoxified, then put through a rehabilitation program whether he likes it or not. Once he's out of the grasp of the drugs, he'll be much more likely to see the benefits of rehab and become a willing participant.

Many addicts, as well, have mental illnesses that make them even less capable of making responsible decisions.

There are those who say we have no right to force people to get their addictions treated, that doing so violates their civil rights.

Sorry. They lose their right to live as drug addicts when they start using our tax money and stealing our property to pay for their addicted lives. And we have a moral duty to step in and help people unable to cope with their problems, an imperative we are presently failing to achieve.

Lack of drug treatment stands as the primary reason for the social catastrophe in the Downtown Eastside, says Al Arsenault, a former Vancouver police officer who worked close to 15 years on Vancouver's skid-row beat.

What Vancouver needs, says Arsenault, won't come cheap.

"The best treatment is the therapeutic-community model," says Arsenault. "That's the solution. Anything else—throwing boxes of needles at somebody—is not the answer. It just keeps people stuck where they are."

While the best examples of the therapeutic-community approach are found in Italy, where success rates top 70 per cent, the model can be applied in B.C. on a scale to fit the need, Arsenault says.

Short-term treatment of 30 to 90 days functions merely as detox, he says.

Addicts in treatment need to be housed under constant supervision, living under rules, sharing in chores and receiving training, education and coaching to prepare for re-integration into society, he says.

"You've got to have long-term treatment," Arsenault says. "It's more expensive but in the long term, it pays off."

Addiction-related costs from policing, the courts, health care, imprisonment and theft are massive, and the loss of productivity adds a huge social and economic cost, he says.

"The loss of human potential is staggering," says Arsenault, a strong advocate for forced rehabilitation who has seen addicts lose limbs to drug-related infections.

"We should say, 'Look, you're losing your arm. You're losing your life. You've lost your job. You've lost your family. So I'm putting you in treatment.'"

Understandably, many law-abiding, taxpaying citizens object to proposals to spend hundreds of millions of dollars setting up and running costly long-term treatment programs for junkies and crack-heads.

But we're already spending almost a million dollars a day on the Downtown Eastside, much of the money going to support addicted lives, while doing little to end the problem. Non-profit social agencies provide important damage control, and save many lives, but the ultimate effect is to keep addicts warehoused in our ghetto, a black hole that sucks in the vulnerable and wrecks their lives.

Without court-imposed long-term addiction treatment, we're going to be spending that million dollars a day forever.

It would be far more cost-effective to invest in rehab programs and facilities that would actually pull people out of that hellhole and back into productive society.

It's easy to judge people who have chosen to destroy their own lives and live off the rest of us. But for those, like Arsenault, who have spent years getting to know the stories behind the addictions, humanity overcomes condemnation.

"I don't judge people for being drug addicts," says Arsenault, a driving force behind the Odd Squad educational films spotlighting addicts in the Downtown Eastside. "I was never date-raped when I was 14. I didn't see my father blow his head off with his shotgun.

"There's some really nice people under the scabs and sores and dirt."

"Cell phone towers, needle exchange, drug addicts," cartoon by Adrian Raeside. Reproduced by permission of Raesidecartoons.com.

At the Welcome Home Society in Surrey, where addicts spend an average of two years getting clean and preparing to become productive citizens, costs run to about $65 a day per resident, or just under $24,000 a year.

Data on success rates are not available because the facility has been operating on a small scale for four years in preparation for an expansion this summer, says director Len Jahn. But those who have graduated so far have done well, Jahn says.

"They're not drains on society," Jahn says. "They're gainfully employed. They're in good, healthy relationships."

To keep someone in a Canadian prison costs nearly three times what it costs to treat an addict at Welcome Home, which is funded primarily by former United Furniture Warehouse owner John Volken.

It's a safe bet that each untreated addict is costing us way more than $24,000 a year in costs related to theft, health care, policing, welfare, jails and the court system.

And each untreated addict represents not only a personal failure, but the failure of our society to assist human beings who cannot help themselves.

Having judges lock them up to clean them up would save us a pile of money, improve thousands of tortured lives and boost the economy.

There's logic in that.

EVALUATING THE AUTHOR'S ARGUMENTS:

Ethan Baron suggests that drug addicts have forfeited their rights and thus deserve to be incarcerated against their will. Do you agree with him? Why or why not? List at least two reasons why you think he is right or two reasons why you think he is wrong.

Viewpoint

4

Drug Addicts Should Be Treated, but Not Locked Up

"'We do things like take syringes out of circulation. . . . Harm reduction is a way of trying to make drug use safer for people who use drugs, without demanding that they stop.'"

Katie Hyslop

In the following viewpoint, Katie Hyslop argues that drug addicts should be treated rather than being incarcerated. She discusses nonincarceration approaches to drug addiction, which include needle-exchange programs, condom-distribution programs, safe drug-consumption sites, and addiction services that give addicts less potent forms of drugs with the goal of weaning them off of drugs entirely. Hyslop says in Canada, where these methods have been tried, rates of drug-abuse-related diseases such as HIV and hepatitis C have significantly declined, while rates of treatment are up. She suggests that treating, rather than criminalizing, drug addiction is key to mitigating the harmful behaviors associated with it.

Hyslop is a writer who lives in Vancouver, British Columbia, Canada.

Hundreds of doctors, politicians, researchers and frontline workers met with drug users and ex-users in Austin, Texas, in December [2010] to openly talk about drug use. But instead of reaffirming their commitment to the decades-long war on drugs, the eighth National Harm Reduction Conference will feature discussions on opening needle exchanges, legalizing and regulating the drug trade, and overdose prevention methods.

The Wisdom of Harm Reduction

"What we do in (the United States) is make drugs as unsafe as they possibly can be, and we do that through laws, which means that, if you get busted with drugs, you go to prison for a long time. And that's designed as a deterrent to make people stop using drugs, which obviously it isn't," said Allan Clear, executive director of the Harm Reduction Coalition, which runs the national conference. "We do things like take syringes out of circulation, which has caused epidemics of hepatitis and HIV. So harm reduction is a way of trying to make drug use safer for people who use drugs, without demanding that they stop using drugs."

Harm reduction can include a range of services from needle exchanges and condom distribution to safe consumption sites and access to addiction services such as methadone and buprenorphine treatments and detox facilities.

Supported by the United Nations and over 93 countries worldwide, harm reduction remains controversial. While over half of the 158 countries where drug use has been reported say they support harm reduction, only 82 countries have needle exchanges, just 73 provide opiate substitution therapies like methadone, and a measly eight countries have safe drug consumption facilities. There are only two safe consumption facilities in North America, both in Vancouver, British Columbia [BC], Canada.

Canada's Success with Harm Reduction

"We were coming to work and people were overdosing and people were dying, and at its height it seemed like it was happening every day, and it just seemed unnecessary. If people were dead, there was no chance of detoxing," said Mark Townsend, executive director of the Portland Hotel Society, which runs Insite, one of the two safe consumption sites in North America, open since 2003.

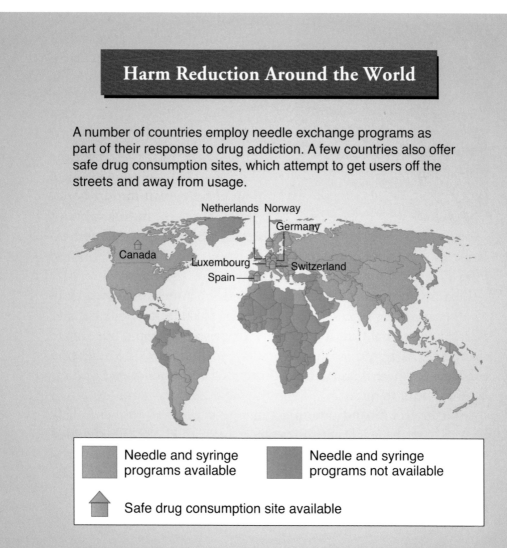

Harm Reduction Around the World

A number of countries employ needle exchange programs as part of their response to drug addiction. A few countries also offer safe drug consumption sites, which attempt to get users off the streets and away from usage.

Netherlands   Norway

Germany

Canada

Luxembourg   Switzerland
Spain

- Needle and syringe programs available
- Needle and syringe programs not available
- Safe drug consumption site available

Taken from: International Harm Reduction Association, "Global State of Harm Reduction 2010: Key Issues for Broadening the Response, 2010," pp. 11–12. www.ihra.net/files/2010/06/29/GlobalState2010_Web.pdf.

"(Insite opened) because lots of people worked hard to make it happen, including the mayor—all the different mayors—and (Premier) Gordon Campbell."

Insite is located in the city's Downtown Eastside, often referred to as Canada's Poorest Postal Code. Injection drug users in that area have a mortality rate 14 times higher than the rest of B.C., with an HIV rate of 4 in 10, and a hepatitis C rate of 9 out of 10 users.

The facility consists of 12 safe-injection booths, monitored by nurses, where clients are provided with clean syringes, cookers, filters, water, and tourniquets, as well as education on safe injection practices that limit the spread of diseases like HIV and hepatitis C. Injection drug use is illegal in Canada, but Insite applied for and received an exemption from the federal government to run the site, though the current government is trying to shut the facility down.

There are approximately 12,000 registered clients at Insite, but in 2009 only 5,447 used the clinic, with an average 491 injections per day. Four-hundred-and-eighty-four overdose interventions were performed that year, with no fatalities—in fact, no one has died at Insite since it opened, but the long lines mean some people walk away without injecting.

Because the local health authority funds it, Insite acts as a gateway to other medical services, such as treating infections and diseases and referrals to mental health treatment. In its second year alone, Insite made 2,000 referrals to outside services, including 800 to addiction counseling. There is also a detox center called Onsite located upstairs if people want to quit.

Vancouver's second safe injection site is less well known, likely because its clientele is limited to people living with HIV/AIDS. Located in the nursing clinic of the Dr. Peter Centre West End, safe injection is only one of the services offered, including access to medication, counseling, and art and music therapy. Unlike Insite, the Dr. Peter Centre has not applied for a government exemption for its safe injection room.

"The College (of Registered Nurses of British Columbia) confirmed for us that it was within the scope of registered nursing practice to supervise injections for two purposes: for the purposes of promoting health and preventing illness. And they went on to say that this is particularly so with a high-risk population," said Maxine Davis, executive director of the Dr. Peter Centre.

Davis estimates there are 50 people out of the clinic's 325 registered patients who inject drugs at the Center. The clinic is only open from 9 a.m. to 3:30 p.m., however, so they also provide people with clean needles to take home, as well as providing a place to have their methadone delivered.

"They Don't Have Any Other Options"

The Canadian federal government opposes safe injection on moral and ethical grounds, and this stance has prevented other Canadian cities from opening their own safe injection sites, including B.C.'s capital city, Victoria. While drug users in Vancouver have access to needle exchanges all over the city, Victoria lost its only fixed-site needle exchange in 2008 after complaints about noise, crimes, garbage and human waste in the area.

The Vancouver Island Health Authority secured another location for the needle exchange in March 2008, but complaints from neighbours resulted in an indefinite hold on a fixed-site needle exchange. Volunteers drive mobile exchange vans in the city, but they have also been banned from that neighbourhood, commonly referred to as the "no-go zone."

"Not having a space where people can be and to feel like they can meet their peers in a safe location is huge. So you have people being very spread out and finding spaces where they can congregate, in spaces that aren't that safe," said Kim Toombs, a member of Harm Reduction Victoria. "People don't want to be using drugs on the street, in front of other people. This is a private thing, and they'd rather be doing it indoors on their own terms, whether it be in their house or whether it be in a safe space. But they're in a position where they don't have any other options."

Less Needle Sharing, Rarer Use

A study released by the city's Centre for Addictions Research this year found that in 2009, 23 per cent of Victoria's drug users reported sharing needles, compared to eight per cent of Vancouver's; 89 per cent of Victoria's users injected daily, compared to 29 per cent of Vancouver's.

Despite the sharp reduction in services to Victoria's drug users, the City of Victoria adopted a harm-reduction policy framework in 2004 and is working on a harm-reduction strategy. The public at large also supports it, with 74 per cent of residents from Victoria and 12 surrounding communities agreeing with harm reduction in Victoria.

Safe Consumption Sites Reduce Disease and Encourage Treatment

The fight for harm-reduction services, particularly needle exchanges and safe consumption sites, has gained ground in both Canada and the United States, but there are still hurdles to overcome.

Despite being the subject of 30 peer-reviewed studies by the BC Centre for Excellence in HIV/AIDS, which showed a significant reduction in public injections and in HIV and hepatitis C infections, as well as an increase in the number of users seeking treatment, Insite is in danger of being shut down by the Canadian federal government, which cites moral and ethical issues with safe injection. After two separate cases before the B.C. Supreme Court and Court of Appeal, which ruled in Insite's favour, the decision now lies with the Supreme Court of Canada.

"The Canadian Medical Association, normally a very conservative body, has stepped in twice to defend Insite, and they will be intervening in the Supreme Court to say, 'This is ridiculous. (Prime Minister) Stephen Harper needs to give his head a shake,'" Townsend said. "You can find an opinion from a fool, but ultimately the information is in and the evidence is utterly clear."

Society Should Be More Sympathetic

It's not just the government that stands in the way, however. Members of the public who don't experience the realities of drug addiction in their lives often do not understand the reason for harm-reduction services, particularly because illicit drug use is illegal in North America.

"We live in a society that doesn't often turn its thoughts to those who are least among us," said Andrew of the Underground Syringe

A harm reduction nurse works with heroin users in Española, New Mexico, providing them with an opiate substitute in exchange for their used syringes.

Exchange of Denver. "And injection drug use affects a very small portion of the population, so, since it's not on their radar, and it's one of those icky topics that they're not interested in delving into because it challenges their moral boundaries. They just kind of look at it and say, 'You know, let 'em die off,' basically."

But Clear of the Harm Reduction Coalition believes it is the politicians, not the public, who are holding back harm reduction, and with the retraction of funding bans on needle exchanges in the United States and the support of safe injection sites by the provincial courts of British Columbia, the future of harm reduction in North America is one of growth.

"The funny thing is that topic opinion polls, the few that exist, have always been pretty consistent that the general public actually supports them. It's not overwhelming, but they are pretty consistent. It's something like 55 to 45, or 52 to 48 in favor of syringe exchange programs. The general public has always been fairly supportive, especially if it's explained what they are for," Clear said.

"And I think that the changing in the legislation around the federal ban on the funding on needle exchange means that some of those programs that have been around for a while, but have not strictly been legal, will be tolerated a lot more by their local health departments. Hopefully we can build upon that, and then they can get funding and be legal and everything."

EVALUATING THE AUTHOR'S ARGUMENTS:

Katie Hyslop reports on programs that aim to reduce drug abuse by providing drug addicts with the means, and even location, to do drugs. Does this seem counterintuitive to you? Why or why not? Explain whether you think the harm-reduction programs described by Hyslop ultimately discourage or encourage drug use, and why.

Facts About Drug Abuse

Editor's note: These facts can be used in reports to add credibility when making important points or claims.

Drug Use in the United States and Around the World

According to the Centers for Disease Control and Prevention (CDC):

- 8 percent of Americans 12 years of age and over have used an illicit drug in the past month.
- 6 percent of Americans 12 years of age and over have used marijuana in the past month.
- 2.5 percent of Americans 12 years of age and over have used a psychotherapeutic drug for a nonmedical purpose in the past month.

The National Survey on Drug Use and Health (NSDUH) reports that about 104 million Americans aged 12 or older have tried marijuana at least once in their lifetimes. That is more than 41 percent of the US population 12 and older.

According to a 2008 World Health Organization (WHO) report on drug use in 17 countries, more Americans have used illegal drugs at some point in their lives than in any other country studied:

Marijuana
1. United States (42.4 percent have used marijuana at some point in their lives)
2. New Zealand (41.9 percent)
3. Netherlands (19.8 percent)
4. France (19 percent)
5. Germany (17.5 percent)
6. Spain (15.9 percent)
7. Israel (11.5 percent)
8. Colombia (10.8 percent)
9. Belgium (10.4 percent)
10. South Africa (8.4 percent)

11. Mexico (7.8 percent)
12. Italy (6.6 percent)
13. Ukraine (6.4 percent)
14. Lebanon (4.6 percent)
15. Nigeria (2.7 percent)
16. Japan (1.5 percent)
17. China (0.3 percent)

Cocaine
1. United States (16.2 percent)
2. New Zealand (4.3 percent)
3. Spain (4.1 percent)
4. Colombia (4 percent)
5. Mexico (4 percent)
6. Germany (1.9 percent)
7. Netherlands (1.9 percent)
8. Belgium (1.5 percent)
9. France (1.5 percent)
10. Italy (1 percent)
11. Israel (0.9 percent)
12. Lebanon (0.7 percent)
13. South Africa (0.7 percent)
14. Nigeria (0.1 percent)
15. Ukraine (0.1 percent)
16. Japan (0.3 percent)
17. China (0 percent)

Teen Drug Use

The 2010 National Survey on Drug Use and Health, published by the Office of Applied Studies (OAS) in the Substance Abuse and Mental Health Services Administration (SAMHSA) found the following about teens and drug abuse:

On an average day during the past year, the following numbers of adolescents aged 12 to 17 used the indicated substances for the first time:
- 7,540 drank alcohol for the first time (10.2 percent of all adolescents).

- 4,365 used an illicit drug for the first time (6 percent of all adolescents).
- 3,845 smoked cigarettes for the first time.
- 3,695 used marijuana for the first time.
- 2,466 used prescription pain relievers nonmedically for the first time.
- 1,406 used hallucinogens for the first time.
- 1,310 used inhalants for the first time.
- 653 used cocaine for the first time.
- 628 used licit or illicit stimulants nonmedically for the first time.
- 127 used methamphetamine for the first time.
- 93 used heroin for the first time.

In the past year:
- 8 million adolescents aged 12 to 17 drank alcohol;
- nearly 5 million used an illicit drug; and
- nearly 4 million smoked cigarettes.

On any given day:
- 1,021,853 adolescents aged 12 to 17 smoke cigarettes;
- 563,182 use marijuana;
- 508,329 drink alcohol;
- 36,572 use inhalants;
- 24,737 use hallucinogens;
- 16,622 use cocaine; and
- 2,866 use heroin.

The Drug Abuse Warning Network (DAWN) estimates that in 2008 there were about a quarter of a million drug-related emergency department (ED) visits by adolescents aged 12 to 17, of which 169,600 visits involved the use of illicit drugs, alcohol, or intentional misuse or abuse of pharmaceuticals (e.g., prescription medicines, over-the-counter remedies, dietary supplements).

On an average day in 2008, there were 723 drug-related ED visits for adolescents aged 12 to 17, of which 465 involved the use of illegal drugs or the misuse or abuse of pharmaceuticals. Of these:

- 151 involved alcohol and no other drug;
- 54 involved alcohol taken together with other drugs;
- 129 involved marijuana;
- 18 involved MDMA (Ecstasy), LSD, PCP, or other hallucinogens;
- 17 involved cocaine;
- 12 involved illicit amphetamines or methamphetamine;
- 6 involved inhalants;
- 5 involved heroin;
- 86 involved prescription or nonprescription pain relievers;
- 31 involved prescription narcotic pain relievers (such as hydrocodone, oxycodone);
- 39 involved benzodiazepines;
- 34 involved antidepressants or antipsychotics;
- 5 involved attention-deficit/hyperactivity disorder (ADHD) medications; and
- 63 were visits for drug-related suicide attempts among adolescents.

American Opinions About Drugs, Drug Laws, and Drug Abuse

A 2011 CNN/Opinion Research poll asked Americans whether they think marijuana should be legalized:
- 41 percent said yes;
- 56 percent said no; and
- 2 percent were unsure.

An October 2010 *Newsweek* poll found the following about American attitudes concerning marijuana legalization:
- 45 percent would support a measure to legalize marijuana in their state.
- 52 percent would oppose it.
- 3 percent were unsure.

- 34 percent support legalizing the use of marijuana to treat certain medical conditions.
- 16 percent do not support legalizing marijuana for medical purposes.
- 4 percent are unsure.

- 46 percent support legalizing all forms of marijuana.
- 73 percent said that if marijuana were to be legalized, they would want it taxed.
- 23 percent said they would not want it taxed.
- 4 percent were unsure.

- 33 percent said that if marijuana were to be legalized, crime would increase.
- 24 percent said that if marijuana were to be legalized, crime would decrease.
- 38 percent said that if marijuana were to be legalized, crime would probably stay about the same
- 5 percent were unsure.

- 36 percent said government-funded health care should cover treatment for marijuana dependence.
- 58 percent said government-funded health care should not cover treatment for marijuana dependence.
- 6 percent were unsure.

A 2010 AP-CNBC Poll found:
- 43 percent of Americans think regulations on marijuana should be more strict than those for alcohol.
- 44 percent of Americans think regulations on marijuana should be the same as those for alcohol.
- 12 percent of Americans think regulations on marijuana should be less strict than those for alcohol.

- 32 percent said legalizing marijuana would improve the economy.
- 21 percent said legalizing marijuana would worsen the economy.
- 46 percent said legalizing marijuana would have no effect on the economy.
- 1 percent were unsure.

- 13 percent said legalizing marijuana would mostly improve the health of people.
- 46 percent said legalizing marijuana would mostly harm the health of people.

- 39 percent said legalizing marijuana would have no effect on the health of people.
- 2 percent were unsure.

- 39 percent said legalizing marijuana would lead more people to use more serious drugs such as heroin and cocaine.
- 10 percent said legalizing marijuana would lead fewer people to use more serious drugs.
- 49 percent said legalizing marijuana would have no effect on how many people use more serious drugs.
- 2 percent were unsure.

Organizations to Contact

The editors have compiled the following list of organizations concerned with the issues debated in this book. The descriptions are derived from materials provided by the organizations. All have publications or information available for interested readers. The list was compiled on the date of publication of the present volume; the information provided here may change. Be aware that many organizations take several weeks or longer to respond to inquiries, so allow as much time as possible for the receipt of requested materials.

American Council for Drug Education (ACDE)
50 Jay St., Brooklyn, NY 11201
(718) 222-6641
e-mail: acde@phoenixhouse.org • website: www.acde.org

The goal of the ACDE is to provide current and effective research to educate the population on drug use and prevention. Programs and services are available to everyone, from employers and educators to students and health care professionals. Students will find a quiz about drug knowledge as well as facts about drugs and their effect on the body.

Canadian Centre on Substance Abuse/Centre canadien de lutte contre l'alcoolisme et les toxicomanies (CCSA/CCLAT)
75 Albert St., Ste. 300, Ottawa, ON K1P 5E7
(613) 235-4048
website: www.ccsa.ca

A Canadian clearinghouse on substance abuse for both English and French speakers, CCSA/CCLAT works to disseminate information on the nature, extent, and consequences of substance abuse and to support and assist organizations involved in substance abuse treatment, prevention, and educational programming. The organization publishes several books, reports, policy documents, brochures, research papers, and newsletters related to alcohol abuse.

Center for Health and Health Care in Schools (CHHCS)
The George Washington University
2121 K St. NW, Ste. 250, Washington, DC 20037
(202) 466-3396 • fax (202) 466-3467
e-mail: chhcs@gwu.edu • website: www.healthinschools.org

Located at The George Washington University School of Public Health, this organization aims to improve the well-being of students across the country by developing health programs in schools. Working closely with educators, school administrators, and health care professionals, the CHHCS strives to ensure that children achieve healthier lives. Its award-winning website offers information for health care professionals, educators, and individuals on a variety of topics related to student drug testing and drug abuse.

Community Anti-Drug Coalitions of America (CADCA)
625 Slaters Ln., Ste. 300, Alexandria, VA 22314
(800) 542-2323 • fax: (703) 706-0565
website: www.cadca.org

CADCA's mission is to help community coalitions create and maintain safe, healthy, and drug-free communities. It was founded in 1992 when organizers began training antidrug coalitions to identify and address drug abuse issues. Now more than five thousand antidrug coalitions can be found throughout the United States. CADCA's website includes information on training and events, as well as interactive media, including blogs, photos, and video.

Drug Free America Foundation, Inc. (DFAF)
5999 Central Ave., Ste. 301, Saint Petersburg, FL 33710
(727) 828-0211 • fax: (727) 828-0212
website: www.dfaf.org

One of the many objectives this United Nations–affiliated organization has is encouraging people to strive for drug-free homes, schools, workplaces, and communities. DFAF focuses on policies and laws that will minimize illegal drug use and drug-related crime. A section of its website is aimed at students and allows them to connect on social networking sites such as Facebook and Twitter.

Drug Policy Alliance (DPA)
70 W. Thirty-Sixth St., 16th Fl., New York, NY 10018
(212) 613-8020 • fax: (212) 613-8021
e-mail: nyc@drugpolicy.org • website: www.drugpolicy.org

One of the DPA's major aims is to educate readers about alternatives in the war against drugs, which it believes to be more detrimental than helpful. It cites the use of science, compassion, health, and human rights as instrumental in its success. The organization recently established a program in New Mexico aimed at teenagers to educate them about issues related to drug abuse.

Drug Reform Coordination Network
1623 Connecticut Ave. NW, 3rd Fl., Washington, DC 20009
(202) 293-8340
e-mail: drcnet@drcnet.org • website: http://stopthedrugwar.org

The Drug Reform Coordination Network opposes the "war on drugs" and works for drug policy reform from a variety of perspectives, including harm reduction, reform of sentencing and forfeiture laws, medicalization of marijuana, and the promotion of an open debate on drug prohibition.

Marijuana Policy Project (MPP)
236 Massachusetts Ave. NE, Ste. 400, Washington, DC 20002
(202) 462-5747
e-mail: info@mpp.org • website: www.mpp.org

The MPP develops and promotes policies to minimize the harm associated with marijuana. It lobbies to reform marijuana laws at the federal level.

National Center on Addiction and Substance Abuse (CASA)
633 Third Ave., 19th Fl., New York, NY 10017-6706
(212) 841-5200
website: www.casacolumbia.org

CASA is a nonprofit organization affiliated with Columbia University in New York City. It works to educate the public about the problems of substance abuse and addiction and to evaluate prevention, treatment, and law enforcement programs established to address the problem. Its website contains reports and op-ed articles on alcohol policy and the alcohol industry.

National Clearinghouse for Alcohol and Drug Information
1 Choke Cherry Rd., Rockville, MD 20857
(877) 726-4727
e-mail: shs@health.org • website: www.health.org

The clearinghouse distributes publications of the US Department of Health and Human Services, the National Institute on Drug Abuse, and other federal agencies concerned with alcohol and drug abuse. Brochure titles include *Tips for Teens About Marijuana.*

National Institute on Drug Abuse (NIDA)
6001 Executive Blvd., Rm. 5213, MSC 9561, Bethesda, MD 20892-9561
(301) 443-6245
e-mail: information@nida.nih.gov • website: www.nida.nih.gov

NIDA supports and conducts research on drug abuse, including the yearly Monitoring the Future survey, to improve addiction prevention, treatment, and policy efforts. It publishes the bimonthly *NIDA Notes* newsletter, the periodic *NIDA Capsules* fact sheets, and a catalog of research reports and public education materials, such as *Marijuana: Facts for Teens* and *Marijuana: Facts Parents Need to Know.*

**National Organization for the Reform
of Marijuana Laws (NORML)**
1600 K St. NW, Washington, DC, 20006
(202) 483-5500
e-mail: norml@norml.org • website: www.normal.org

NORML fights to legalize marijuana and to help those who have been convicted and sentenced for possessing or selling marijuana. In addition to pamphlets and position papers, it publishes the newsletter *Marijuana Highpoints,* the bimonthly *Legislative Bulletin* and *Freedom@NORML,* and the monthly *Potpourri.*

National Scholastic Anti-Doping Program (NSADP)
8730 Big Bend Blvd., St. Louis, MO 63119
(314) 963-3404
website: www.nsadp.com

The NSADP was created to develop a complete steroid educational package and testing program. It employs certified antidoping officers to conduct testing, a certified medical review officer (MRO) to review all test results, and computer technology to assure confidentiality and accuracy of all testing data. The NSADP works directly with the UCLA Olympic Testing Lab, the only World Anti-Doping Association–certified laboratory in the United States.

Office of National Drug Control Policy (ONDCP)
PO Box 6000
Rockville, MD 20849-6000
(800) 666-3332
e-mail: ondcp@ncjrs.org • website: www.whitehousedrugpolicy.gov

The ONDCP is responsible for formulating the government's national drug strategy and the president's antidrug policy as well as coordinating the federal agencies responsible for stopping drug trafficking. Drug policy studies are available upon request.

Partnership for a Drug-Free America
352 Park Ave. S, 9th Fl., New York, NY 10010
(212) 922-1560
website: www.drugfreeamerica.org

The Partnership for a Drug-Free America is a nonprofit organization that utilizes media communication to reduce demand for illicit drugs in America. Best known for its national antidrug advertising campaign, the partnership works to "unsell" drugs to children and to prevent drug use among kids.

Students Against Destructive Decisions (SADD)
255 Main St., Marlborough, MA 01752
(877) 723-3462
e-mail: info@sadd.org • website: www.sadd.org

Originally called Students Against Drunk Driving, SADD's mission later expanded to provide students with the best prevention and intervention tools possible to deal with the issues of underage drinking, other drug use, impaired driving, and other destructive decisions. SADD's website has statistics on teens and drunk driving along with information on how to form local SADD chapters.

Students for Sensible Drug Policy (SSDP)
1623 Connecticut Ave. NW, Ste. 300, Washington, DC 20009
(202) 293-4414 • fax: (202) 293-8344
e-mail: ssdp@ssdp.org • website: www.ssdp.org

The SSDP is built around a network of students who in turn encourage other students to become active in the political process related to drug policy. In particular, they seek to change policies that are most detrimental to students. This is a grassroots organization, and students around the country are encouraged to start their own local chapter of SSDP, thus learning the important issues surrounding activism.

**Substance Abuse and Mental Health Services
Administration (SAMHSA)**
**National Clearinghouse for Alcohol and
Drug Information (NCADI)**
PO Box 2345, Rockville, MD 20847-2345
(800) 729-6686
website: http://ncadi.samhsa.gov/

SAMHSA is the division of the US Department of Health and Human Services that is responsible for improving the lives of those with or at risk for mental illness or substance addiction. Through the NCADI, SAMHSA provides the public with a wide variety of information on alcoholism and other addictions.

US Department of Education, Office of Safe and Drug-Free Schools (OSDFS)
550 Twelfth St. SW, 10th Fl., Washington, DC 20202
(202) 245-7896 • fax: (202) 485-0013
e-mail: osdfs.safeschl@ed.gov
website: www.ed.gov/about/offices/list/osdfs

This organization strives to bring drug education and assistance with creating drug-free policies to schools and universities across the United States. There is a heavy emphasis on drug prevention both at the state and national level. Its website provides information about national and state programs, reports, and news related to creating safe and drug-free schools.

US Drug Enforcement Administration (DEA)
8701 Morrissette Dr., Springfield, VA 22152
(202) 307-1000
website: www.dea.gov

Founded by President Richard Nixon in 1973, the DEA was created for the purpose of waging a war on the problem of drug abuse. More than three decades later, the DEA employs more than five thousand agents and has outposts in more than sixty countries around the world. Its mission remains to enforce laws related to controlled substances. The DEA aims to bring to justice people who grow, manufacture, or distribute illegal drugs. The DEA website includes information for young adults about drug prevention.

For Further Reading

Books

Benavie, Arthur. *Drugs: America's Holy War.* New York: Routledge, 2008. Explores the impact and cost of America's war on drugs both financially and on people. Argues that ending the drug war would have multiple international benefits, destroy dangerous and illegal drug cartels, and allow the American government to more positively focus its resources and attention.

Geluardi, John. *Cannabiz: The Explosive Rise of the Medical Marijuana Industry.* Sausalito, CA: Polipoint, 2010. Explores the history, economics, health, and the politics of the medical marijuana movement and burgeoning industry.

Gibler, John. *To Die in Mexico: Dispatches from Inside the Drug War.* San Francisco: City Lights, 2011. Tells behind-the-scenes stories that address the causes and consequences of Mexico's multibillion-dollar drug trafficking business.

Grim, Ryan. *This Is Your Country on Drugs: The Secret History of Getting High in America.* Hoboken, NJ: Wiley, 2010. Explores the evolution of drug use in America and criticizes antidrug programs and other policy decisions.

Kleiman, Mark A.R., Jonathan P. Caulkins, and Angela Hawken. *Drugs and Drug Policy: What Everyone Needs to Know.* Oxford: Oxford University Press, 2011. Examines the role of drugs in US foreign policy, their relationship to terrorism, and the politics that surround the issue.

Reding, Nick. *Methland: The Death and Life of an American Small Town.* New York: Bloomsbury USA, 2010. Offers a powerful and terrifying look at the drug epidemic in America's heartland by examining a small town's methamphetamine use and production.

Regan, Trish. *Joint Ventures: Inside America's Almost Legal Marijuana Industry.* Hoboken, NJ: Wiley, 2011. Discusses how pot has moved out of the shadows and into the mainstream and the dispensaries that have resulted from the trend. Examines the domestic and international pot-smuggling trade and assesses its many costs, from gang violence and big profits for criminals to billions of dollars in lost tax revenues, and the potential boon of legalization to local economies across the nation.

Robinson, Matthew B., and Renee G. Scherlen. *Lies, Damned Lies, and Drug War Statistics: A Critical Analysis of Claims Made by the Office of National Drug Control Policy.* Albany: State University of New York Press, 2007. Analyzes claims made by the Office of National Drug Control Policy (ONDCP), the White House agency of accountability in the nation's drug war. Argues that the ONDCP manipulates statistics.

Periodicals and Internet Sources

Akst, Daniel. "Portugal Shows Way to Decriminalize Drug Possession," *Winnipeg Free Press,* March 12, 2011. www.winnipeg freepress.com/opinion/westview/portugal-shows-way-to-decrimi nalize-drug-possession-117847848.html.

Backstrom, James C. "Marijuana, America's Most Dangerous Illegal Drug," *MPR News,* June 21, 2010. http://minnesota.publicradio .org/display/web/2010/06/21/backstrom.

Balko, Radley. "Should We Allow Performance Enhancing Drugs in Sports?," *Reason,* January 23, 2008. http://reason.com /archives/2008/01/23/should-we-allow-performance-en.

Benedictus, Leo. "How the British Fell Out of Love with Drugs," *Guardian* (Manchester, UK), February 24, 2011. www.guardian .co.uk/society/2011/feb/24/british-drug-use-falling.

Boniface, Dan, and Dan Weaver. "Weighing the Benefits of Medical Marijuana," 9News.com (Denver, CO), April 30, 2010. www.9news.com/rss/story.aspx?storyid=137842.

Bowker, Art. "The 21st Century Substance Abuser: Cyberspace Intersecting with the Drug Culture," *Corrections,* March 21, 2011. www.corrections.com/news/article/28224-the-21st-century-sub stance-abuser-cyberspace-intersecting-with-the-drug-culture.

Byrd, Cary. "The Internet Is Not the Cause of Prescription Drug Abuse," PRWeb, May 27, 2008. www.prweb.com/releases/Internet -pharmacy/prescription-drugs/prweb969324.htm.

Carey, Nick. "America's New Touchy-Feely 'War on Drugs,'" Reuters, January 21, 2010. www.reuters.com/article/2010/01/21/us-drugs -usa-consumption-idUSTRE60K63G20l00121?pageNumber=1.

Conant, Eve. "Pot and the GOP," *Newsweek,* October 25, 2010. www.newsweek.com/2010/10/25/the-conservative-case-for-legal izing-pot.html.

Dalrymple, Theodore. "It Is Right to Imprison Drug Addicts," *Social Affairs Unit,* March 18, 2008. www.socialaffairsunit.org.uk/blog /archives/001744.php.

DuPont, Robert L. "Why We Should Not Legalize Marijuana," CNBC Special Report: "Marijuana and Money," April 20, 2010. www .cnbc.com/id/36267223.

Economist. "Stay Out of Jail Clean," February 24, 2011. www.econo mist.com/node/18233647.

Faulkner, Katherine. "Alcohol 'More Dangerous than Crack, Heroin and Ecstasy,'" *MailOnline,* November 1, 2010. www.dailymail .co.uk/health/article-1325472/Professor-David-Nutt-Alcohol -harmful-heroin-crack-Ecstasy.html.

Freeman, Marc. "Random Tests Credited with Reducing Drug Use Among High-School Athletes," Sun-Sentinel.com, January 2, 2011. http://articles.sun-sentinel.com/2011-01-02/news/fl-random -drug-testing-athletes-20101231_1_random-drug-testing-screen ing-for-illegal-drugs-nms-management-services.

Goodnough, Abby, and Katie Zezima. "Newly Born, and Withdrawing from Painkillers," *New York Times,* April 9, 2011. www.nytimes .com/2011/04/10/us/10babies.html?_r=1&ref=us.

Gumbiner, Jann. "Is Marijuana Addictive?," *Psychology Today,* December 5, 2010. www.psychologytoday.com/blog/the-teenage -mind/201012/is-marijuana-addictive.

Harpring, James G. "Is America Winning the War on Drugs? Yes," *TC Palm* (Florida), May 20, 2009. www.tcpalm.com/news/2009 /may/20/james-g-harpring-pro-con-america-winning-war-drugs/.

Harvard Mental Health Letter. "Medical Marijuana and the Mind," April 2010. www.health.harvard.edu/newsletters/Harvard _Mental_Health_Letter/2010/April/ medical-marijuana-and-the -mind.

International Narcotics Control Board. *Report of the International Narcotics Control Board for 2010,* United Nations Publication E/INCB/2010/1, March 2, 2011. www.incb.org/pdf/annual -report/2010/en/AR_2010_Chapter_III_Americas.pdf.

Jenkins, Simon. "Our War on Drugs Has Been an Abysmal Failure," *Guardian* (Manchester, UK), September 9, 2010. www.guardian .co.uk/commentisfree/cifamerica/2010/sep/09/war-on-drugs-legal isation.

McClain, Dani. "Media Hype About Painkillers Shot Down," *WireTap,* April 30, 2007. www.wiretapmag.org/rights/43089.

Mendoza, Martha. "U.S. War on Drugs Has Met None of Its Goals," *Huffington Post,* May 13, 2010. www.huffingtonpost .com/2010/05/13/us-war-on-drugs-has-met-n_n_575351 .html?ref=fb&src=sp.

PBS. "Doping for Gold: The Dangers of Doping," *Secrets of the Dead,* May 6, 2008. www.pbs.org/wnet/secrets/features/doping-for-gold /the-dangers-of-doping/56/.

Seppa, Nathan. "Not Just a High," *Science News,* June 19, 2010. www.sciencenews.org/view/feature/id/59872/title/Not_just_a _high.

StateNews (Michigan State University), "Ban on K2 Is a Politically Expedient Overreaction," editorial, September 26, 2010. www .statenews.com/index.php/article/2010/09/ban_on_k2_is_a _politically_expedient_overreaction.

Szalavitz, Maia. "Outlawing Legal Highs: Can Emergency Bans Hinder Drug Development?," *Healthland* (blog), *Time,* February 23, 2011. http://healthland.time.com/2011/02/23/outlawing -legal-highs-can-emergency-bans-hinder-drug-development.

Thomas, Pierre, and Lisa Jones. "Synthetic Marijuana: 'Legal' High a Dangerous Thrill for Young Americans," ABC News, November 22, 2010. http://abcnews.go.com/US/synthetic-marijuana-legal -drug-scary-consequences/story?id=12211253.

Vela, José Julio. "Getting Sober: Feds Attempt to Crack Down on Internet Drug Pushers," *Health Law Perspectives,* University of Houston, April 2010. www.law.uh.edu/healthlaw/perspec tives/2010/(JV)%20Internet.pdf.

Websites

D.A.R.E. (www.dare.com). This is the website of the antidrug program, Drug Abuse Resistance Education, better known as D.A.R.E. The site contains useful information about drugs, drug abuse, and prevention strategies.

Harm Reduction International (www.ihra.net). This organization promotes policies and practices that reduce the harm associated with drug abuse. An example of a harm-reduction strategy would be providing a space where addicts can use drugs in a safe and clean way. The group's website discusses its very controversial philosophy and offers information on programs worldwide.

NIDA for Teens (http://teens.drugabuse.gov). This site, published and maintained by the National Institute on Drug Abuse, is geared toward issues and questions young people have about drugs and drug abuse.

Index

National Survey on Drug Use and Health (NSDUH), 14, 28, 50, 59

Needle exchange programs, countries with, *111*

NIDA (National Institute on Drug Abuse), 29, 34, 49

NSDUH (National Survey on Drug Use and Health), 14, 28, 50, 59

Nutt, David, 78

O

OAI (Operation All Inclusive), 92, 94

Obama, Barack, 61

Office of National Drug Control Policy (ONDCP), 19

O'Malley, Patrick M., 11

ONDCP (Office of National Drug Control Policy), 19

1-pentyl-3-(1-naphthoyl)indole (K9, JWH018), 84, 86
See also Synthetic marijuana

Operation All Inclusive (OAI), 92, 94

Operation Xcellerator, 90–91

Opiates (opioids)
fatal poisonings from, 27
global consumption of, 99

Opinion polls. *See* Surveys

Oxycontin, 28
percentage of past year use among 12th graders, *30*
survey of 10th graders on ease of obtaining, 29

Oz, Mehmet, 8, 9, 64

P

Pain relievers, prescription, 26, 28, 29
emergency room visits due to, 27
numbers seeking treatment for abuse of, *35*

Paredes-Cordova, Jorge Mario, 94

Parents' Movement, 23

Performance-enhancing drug(s), *40*
abuse is serious problem in sports, 37–42
states mandating testing of student athletes for, 41
use should be allowed in sports, 43–47

Polls. *See* Surveys

Prescription drug abuse
extent of, has been exaggerated, 32–36
is skyrocketing, 25–31
percentage of past year use among 12th graders, by drug, *30*
prevalence among 12th graders, 15–16

Project Reckoning, *91,* 91–92

R

Ramirez, Manny, 38

Rannazzisi, Joseph, 41, 42

Reagan, Nancy, 23

Reefer Madness (film), 58

Riggs, Micah, 86

Rivera-Perez, Juan, 94

Rodriguez, Alex, 38

Roizen, Mike, 64
Roosevelt, Franklin D., 58
Ryan, Mark, 7

S
SAMHSA (Substance Abuse
   and Mental Health Services
   Administration), 14, 51
Sampels, Kristy, 7
Sanders, Dickie, 8
Saunders, Richard, 8, 9
Schaefer, Kurt, 85
Schizophrenia, marijuana use
   and, 50, 53
Schulenberg, John E., 11
Schultz, George, 60, 98
Selig, Bud, 45
Sinaloa Cartel, 90–91
Sosa, Sammy, 47
Spice (synthetic marijuana), *79,*
   86
   bans on, are ineffective,
      82–87
   opinion on legislation
      banning, *84*
   should be banned, 77–81
   states banning, *80*
Sports
   performance-enhancing-drug
      abuse is serious problem in,
      37–42
   use of performance-enhancing
      drugs should be allowed in,
      43–47
Steroids. *See* Anabolic-
   androgenic steroids
Stewart, David, 7
Stimulants, 26, 28

emergency room visits due to,
   27, 29
numbers seeking treatment
   for abuse of, *35*
percentage of past year use
   among 12th graders, *30*
Substance Abuse and
   Mental Health Services
   Administration (SAMHSA),
   14, 51
Surveys
   on approval of medical
      marijuana, 73, *75*
   on banning synthetic
      marijuana, *84*
   on legalization of marijuana,
      54, 61–62
   on lifetime use of any illicit
      drug among students, *15*
   on prevalence of marijuana
      use among youth, 60
   of 10th graders on ease of
      obtaining OxyContin, 29
   on 12th graders' disapproval
      of steroids, 42
   on use of cocaine/inhalants/
      LSD among 12th graders,
      20
   of youth on ease of obtaining
      marijuana, 14
Sweetingham, Lisa, 37
Synthetic marijuana, *79*
   bans on, are ineffective,
      82–87
   should be banned, 77–81

T
Tinajero, Jorge Hernández, 98

Tobacco, number of deaths
   from, 34
Toombs, Kim, 113
Townsend, Mark, 111, 114
Treatment
   admissions for alcohol *vs.*
      pain killer abuse, 36
   numbers seeking, by
      substance, *35*
   as part of US drug policy,
      21–22

U
University of British Columbia,
   73
University of California Center
   for Medicinal Cannabis
   Research, 70
Urbina-Amaya, Luis, 94

V
Vicodin, 14, 28
   percentage of past year use
      among 12th graders, *30,*
      34
Volcker, Paul, 98
Volken, John, 107
Volkow, Nora D., 25

W
War on drugs
   funding for, *100*
   has been successful, 89–96
   is a failure, 97–101

Z
Zagier, Alan Scher, 82
Zedillo, Ernesto, 98
Zolpidem (Ambien), 27

Picture Credits

© AJPhoto/Photo Researchers, Inc., 22, 33

© AP Images/The Ames Tribune, Andrew Rullestad, 61

© AP Images/The Clarion Ledger, Joe Ellis, 86

© AP Images/The Journal and Constitution, Joey Ivansco, 91

© AP Images/Kelly McCall, 79

© AP Images/Rich Pedroncelli, 71

© AP images/The Santa Fe New Mexican, Luis Sanchez Saturno, 115

© AP Images/Nick Ut, 48

© F1online digitale Bildagentur GmbH/Alamy, 104

© Robert Galbraith/Reuters/Landov, 88

Gale/Cengage Learning, 15, 20, 30, 35, 39, 54, 62, 75, 80, 84, 93, 100, 111

© imagebroker/Alamy, 52

© Kuttig-People/Alamy, 13

© Publiphoto/Photo Researchers, Inc., 10

© Sabrina Rummell/Alamy, 27

© Time & Life Pictures/Getty Images, 46

© Universal TempSport/Corbis, 40

© Rick Wilking/Reuters/Landov, 65